IN FILIAL DISOBEDIENCE

*'Filialiter et obedienter non obedio,
contradico et rebello'*

ROBERT GROSSETESTE

by

ADRIAN HASTINGS

MAYHEW-McCRIMMON
Great Wakering

First published in Great Britain in 1978 by
MAYHEW-McCRIMMON
Great Wakering, Essex, England

ISBN 0 85597 249 1

Acknowledgements:
  "Can the Pope be wrong? Humanae Vitae and the Church"
was first published in 1968 by Burns & Oates as "The Papacy
and the Church", used here with permission of Search Press.
  "The Right to Rule" was given as a lecture in 1975 at an
ecumenical conference of the *Church Society,* Wycliffe Hall,
Oxford, and published in the Churchman, used here with per-
mission.
  "The Right to the Cup" was first published in "The Tablet" in
February 1977 used here with permission of the Tablet
Publishing Company.
  "The Triangle of Salvation" first appeared as in Gaba
Pastoral Institute 1972, also used here with permission.

Printed by Mayhew-McCrimmon Ltd, Great Wakering,
Essex, England

Contents

Preface   9

PART I

1. The right to marry – the priesthood and celibacy   13
2. A history of my religious development   25

PART II

3. Can the Pope be wrong? *Humanae Vitae*   121
   and the Church
4. The right to rule – recent developments in the   136
   Catholic Church
5. The right to celebrate – sharing the cup   156
6. The triangle of salvation   163

'It is the custom with Protestant writers to consider that, whereas there are two great principles in action in the history of religion, Authority and Private Judgement, they have all the Private Judgement to themselves, and we have the full inheritance and the superincumbent oppression of Authority. But this is not so; it is the vast Catholic body itself, and it only, which affords an arena for both combatants in that awful, never-dying duel. It is necessary for the very life of religion, viewed in its large operations and its history, that the warfare should be incessantly carried on.'

John Henry Newman
Apologia Pro Vita Sua.

Adrian Hastings

By the same author

White domination or racial peace, the Africa Bureau, 1954.

Prophet and witness in Jerusalem, a study of the teaching of St. Luke, Longmans, 1958.

The church and the nations, ed., Sheed & Ward, 1959.

One and apostolic, Darton, Longman & Todd, 1963.

The world mission of the church, Darton, Longman & Todd, 1964.

Church and mission in modern Africa, Burns & Oates, 1967.

A concise guide to the documents of the second Vatican Council, Darton, Longman & Todd, two volumes, 1968 and 1969.

Mission and Ministry, Sheed & Ward, 1971.

Church and Ministry, Gaba Publications, Uganda, 1972.

Christian Marriage in Africa, SPCK, 1973.

Wiriyamu, Search Press, 1974.

Southern Africa and the christian conscience, Catholic Institute for International Relations, 1975.

The Faces of God, Geoffrey Chapman, 1975.

African Christianity, Geoffrey Chapman, 1976.

Bishops and writers, aspects of the evolution of modern English catholicism, ed., Anthony Clarke. 1977.

Preface

When last summer I came to the decision to reject the canonical obligation of celibacy I realised that this involved providing a clear public explanation of what I was doing and why. In October, as a consequence, I completed the statement published in *New Blackfriars* for March which appears as chapter 1 of this book. Having written this, I felt that it was not really enough, or at least that my friends and readers of my previous books could be helped if I placed this decision as frankly as seemed reasonable within a wider context of my own life and my understanding of the Church. The first I have tried to do in chapter 2, written during November and December. As regards the second, I have retaken in the second half of the book with slight amendments four pieces previously published. Chapter 3 was my immediate response to the encyclical *Humanae Vitae* written in the tense summer of 1968. Chapter 4 was given as a lecture to an ecumenical conference of the *Church Society* at Wycliffe Hall,

Oxford, in September 1975. Chapter 5 reflects a decision taken just a year ago and published in the *Tablet*. Chapter 6 was first printed in 1972 at Gaba Pastoral Institute, Uganda, as part of a book entitled *Church and Ministry*. The mood of these four pieces, written over the space of nearly ten years and in rather differing circumstances, naturally varies. Nevertheless they present, I believe, a fairly consistent, if developing, view of the Church and of the rights and duties of church members. It is within this view that the present decision has been taken.

The impression received by the reader from all this may well be that of an obstinately 'rebel priest'. In some sense that would, undeniably, be fair enough. Certainly I here contest, and pretty sharply, many of the current policies of our ecclesiastical leadership as well as some of their underlying presuppositions. Yet I would still hope that a deeper impression would be of someone who is far too seriously concerned for the life and growth of the Church to be written off as a rebel. Perhaps indeed I have loved the Catholic Church altogether too much, but at least despite a thousand warts I have found in it a home possessed of such riches as I do not believe to exist elsewhere upon this earth. But because it is my home and has always been so, I feel a free citizen within it. *Civis Romanus sum.* More than fifteen years ago, it could be said, Chairman John opened the windows of the Catholic Church that, after centuries of stuffiness, a thousand new flowers might bloom beside and above the thousand warts. This book is my personal response and tribute to Pope John, my withstanding to the face those who with the best of intentions would restrict our freedom to let the flowers bloom.

The decision I have taken is, I believe, for my own happiness too. There are personal dimensions to one's life which there is no reason to speak of even in so personal a book as this. They are very much there but they have not, I hope, trespassed destructively or irrationally upon the more objective and impersonal themes of my thinking, hard as it can be to hold both in rein. Rather, over the long years the two have gradually coalesced so that it is finally impossible wholly to disentangle them. The struggle to go on relating one's life to an evolving vision of the true and the good without either insensitively betraying past commitments or continuing to adhere outwardly (perhaps all too cynically) to things no longer honestly believed in, is a hard one for any man. But there is really no alternative if one is to keep one's integrity. This little book is as a whole an attempt to show the way one man, a believing christian of the Catholic communion, has faced that struggle. If it has been a self-deceiving or self-seeking way, would the gentle reader still generously pray for me that – despite all – in words Thomas More used in the last of his letters to Margaret Roper, 'we maie merily meete in heaven'.

Finally, I must thank those who have helped me in coming to this decision, particularly members of my family who have gently but firmly questioned my arguments, my sister Susan especially. Most of all I must thank my mother who has provided unfailing understanding and support through months of much stress and typed the greater part of chapter 2.

It is worth stressing at the end of this preface that in challenging the law of celibacy I do not, and could not, challenge the worth of celibacy itself, unpopular as that may be in today's world. Poor is the Church in which there are no celibates, ordained or unordained, men or women, who have freely embraced this aspect of the lifestyle of Jesus and Paul. Its creativity in age after age has been unbounded – the creativity of a Benedict, a Francis of Assisi, a Theresa of Avila (incidentally, none of whom was ordained). Celibacy shines, it seems to me, in quality rather than in quantity. In freedom it can provide a spiritual liberation and commitment immeasurably valuable both for those who choose it and for the wider society. I owe so much personally to saintly and beloved priests and nuns I have known that I would be ungrateful indeed to 'attack' celibacy as I have been accused of doing. May the flowers of celibacy bloom beside the flowers of marriage, and may they both be the flowers of the priesthood as they are both the flowers of the unordained. *Aggiornamento* can settle for no less.

ADRIAN HASTINGS

1

The Right to Marry

After much thought and prayer I have come to the decision that I am free as a Catholic priest to marry. I have come to this after long years of wrestling with myself and of pondering both the pastoral and missionary needs of the Church and the basic nature of the Christian priesthood, marriage and freedom. I have for years argued persistently for a major change in the Church's position in this regard, a change which I see as absolutely crucial for the wider effectiveness and coherence of the *aggiornamento* set in motion by Pope John. It is only recently that I have come to the conclusion that in this matter as in others one cannot go on indefinitely simply affirming in print and in speech a point of view completely at odds with the structured ordering of one's own life. There comes a moment when it is morally necessary to pin oneself to the truth and importance of what one has affirmed to be true and important.

I have been a priest for 22 years. I accepted the obligation of celibacy at ordination without questioning because I wished to be a priest and this was the law of the Church, and I have kept it. In the cheerful, zealous, withdrawn atmosphere of a seminary it did not seem much of a problem. I was even convinced for a time that I did not want to marry, but for many years now I have wanted to very much. So this decision is first of all a response to an honest sense of my own need. Yet at present I am living happily with my mother; I have many dear friends, and I am extremely busy as a university lecturer and writer. I have certainly not come to this decision out of loneliness or depression or because I have lost interest in the Church or the Catholic priesthood. Quite the contrary.

I first became firmly convinced that the Church needed to change its discipline about 15 years ago and so I wrote in the *African Ecclesiastical Review* of October 1964 urging the widespread ordination of tried and tested married men, such as the better trained catechists, to provide the Eucharist and the simple preaching of the Gospel. From then on I have repeated this appeal time after time in every way open to me, explaining at great lengths the grounds for it (see, for instance, the *Clergy Review*, January-March 1973; the *Tablet*, 8 and 15 May, 1976), but over the years I have seen that what I first asked for was certainly not enough. Reasons which called for a married priesthood appeared to my mind of an ever wider and more compelling kind: but for long I continued to hold that, whatever my personal inclinations, I must myself remain celibate precisely to put the case. Thus on the 5th October 1969 I copied down a remark of von Hügel's into my diary: 'Whatever one may think, *in abstracto*, of celibacy, a priest who abandons it puts himself out of court for pleading for the difficult reforms we require.' Hard as it might be to order one's own life by a rule one did not believe in, I was for long firmly convinced that in practice this settled the matter for me. On this, after almost interminable internal debate, I have changed my mind: partly because I am tired of having my own life controlled by a clericalism I detest; partly because verbal argument alone, however clearly put, is very easily disregarded by the powers that be. The very absence of democracy within the Church as it stands drives one from disregarded argumentation to deeds that may not be so easily forgotten.

I have recently celebrated the 22nd anniversary of my ordination and the 40th of my first communion. I made that communion at Stanbrook Abbey on the feast of Our Lady's birthday, the 8th September 1937. On its 40th anniversary I was back at Stanbrook to thank God for all those years of receiving and communicating the Body of Christ, that food in whose strength I have walked for forty years. And in doing so I felt a profound sense of reassurance. These have been the central things in my life. From them I do not, will not, could not, withdraw.

How then could I break a law of the Church forbidding me to marry, a law which I accepted with full consciousness when I was ordained in 1955? Because I do not believe it to be a just law or a good law, or a law which the Church had the right to make, and I am convinced that it does not express God's will for the Church today, if it ever did. Positive law is not to be despised but equally it is not to be idolised, and this applies very much indeed to canon law which is often made and enforced in a very arbitrary manner. Law is for man, not man for it. I am the son and grandson of lawyers, and I have always held human law in the greatest respect; but the free conscientious, non-violent breaking of a law which is itself proving harmful and destructive, can be a valuable and redeeming action. So, at least, it would seem to me the Christ of the gospels teaches us. I accepted the law of compulsory priestly celibacy when young as an expression of God's will; convinced today that it is, on the contrary, a grave disservice to the

Kingdom, I can contemplate breaking it without any sense of failing in fidelity to the God who has guarded, guided and blessed me all the days of my life.

The practicalities of this decision have been helped by the fact that I am now a university lecturer in religious studies. As a missionary of sorts, an itinerant minister, there were very good reasons to be celibate, and I could hold freely to my celibacy because it made much sense in terms of the work I was actually given. That period of my life has now past. As a university lecturer marriage appears as appropriate as celibacy did for a traveller living mostly far from his native land and on next to no salary. If the Church had given me other responsibilities I would not have wished to abandon them lightly and so let people down who depended on my immediate ministry, but it did not do so. As a consequence I find I have the responsibility instead to use my freedom in a way most other priests cannot do, to say something utterly vital about the priesthood without the likelihood of being immediately crushed.

I intend then, whether or not I marry, to continue with the grace of God to be a priest in the depths of my being and to serve as such as God guides me. That service has long been chiefly one of teaching through writing, and so it will continue. I have not the slightest desire to divide the Church sacramentally. There are in fact recognised married priests in the Catholic Church today, as there always have been, so there can be no scandal in a married man celebrating Mass. But I will certainly not do so except when I am truly wanted and such celebration is not divisive.

What, then, objectively are my reasons for taking this very grave decision? The first reason, and still for me in a way the clearest, is the simple and decisive one of the pastoral needs of the Church. The Church is centred upon the Mass. The Eucharistic Body of Christ builds up the

Mystical Body of Christ. No theology is more traditional and nothing was stressed more repeatedly by the second Vatican Council. It has, ever since my doctoral thesis in Rome in the 1950s, been central to my own theology (see *One and Apostolic,* London and New York, 1963; *A Concise Guide to the Documents of the Second Vatican Council,* volume I, 1968). The whole weight of the Catholic tradition and spirituality cries out for the celebration of the Lord's Supper on the Lord's Day in every christian community. But this, as I experienced over long years in Africa, has become utterly impossible because of the great and growing lack of priests. It is not that there are not devoted people, trained ministers of the Church, available. There are. In Africa, for instance, the Church has many thousands of capable catechists, but they are married. The celebration of Mass in rural Africa today, despite the quickly growing number of Catholics, is an increasingly rare event. Many bishops have seen this absolutely clearly and have appealed to the Pope time after time for permission to ordain married men 'to answer the most elementary pastoral needs' (The joint hierarchies of Gabon, Chad, the Central African Republic, Congo-Brazza and Cameroon in July 1969). One bishop I know went year after year to plead for this in Rome always to be faced with the same hard refusal, though he had not a single ordained local priest in his diocese. The Pope, it seems, prefers that there be no Mass for countless people than that Mass be said by a married man, and so no Mass there is. It is spiritually very comfortable for me to go on saying Mass in common with all the priests and bishops in their private chapels who are never deprived for a day of the Eucharist, but I have found it increasingly impossible to accept such an identification with the clerical 'haves'.

All this is equally true and has very long been true of Latin America. Today it is becoming the case in many parts of France and Germany. Whatever the underlying reasons the consequence is to reveal ever more clearly an order of priorities dominated by a clericalism which sees the maintenance of a universal priestly celibacy as more important than the basic pastoral and missionary needs of the Church. Such a state of affairs has become in my opinion a scandal of the highest order.

But the pastoral needs of today's Church by no means end there. Despite pressure from Rome through the ages the Eastern Uniate Churches have managed to maintain their ancient tradition of a married clergy to this day. However, millions of Uniates have emigrated from Eastern Europe to America and there they have been forbidden to continue this tradition and so have been alienated and frequently driven into schism. Again in the last years since the Council there have been deep conflicts between Rome and the Melkites and Ukrainian Catholics, and these largely relate to the refusal of Rome to allow a married clergy to develop in North America. Such a policy damages the tribute the Vatican Council paid to the eastern churches, maintains a continuing open wound within the Church, and counteracts any further ecumenical proposal to bring Anglicans or Protestants into full communion with the Catholic Church on some sort of uniate model. Papal pronouncements about the acceptance of the legitimate rights and traditions of other churches as part of the process of achieving full communion can appear as little more than double-talk when, within the Catholic Church as already constituted, a married clergy, characteristic of all other denominations, is so consistently resisted by authority. One cannot reasonably offer with one hand what one is refusing with the other.

Again, there are the lands where the Church is, and for many years has been, under persecution. In such countries it can be quite impossible to provide a celibate clergy only ordainable after long years of traditional seminary formation. As the priests of the diocese of Vilkaviskis, Lithuania, movingly petitioned their bishops in December 1968: 'The present seminary is obviously unable to fulfil the needs of the Lithuanian Catholic Church. Therefore a well-justified question arises: Who in the near future will proclaim God's Word? Who will give the Sacraments? Who will officiate at the Mass?' If the law of universal priestly celibacy remains in force, the answer to those questions may well be 'No one'.

Here in Britain there are now scores of priests who have married but wish to continue their ministry. In France there are hundreds, 'prêtres en foyer' they call them, and many are saying Mass while the bishops avert their eyes. These are good men, some of them were among the best and ablest of the clergy, men who often enough went out with a quite particular zeal to preach the word and serve the needy in a secular world far away from that of the presbytery. It is a wretched experience to see one's friends leave the ministry and the bishops do next to nothing about it.

My conclusion is a simple one: in Britain, France and Germany, in Lithuania, among the Melkites in north America, in Africa, in Latin America, wherever one turns, the clericalism which puts celibacy above ministry is strangling the Church.

Yet there is absolutely no reliable theological argument upon which to base a general law of priestly celibacy (which is, maybe, why there is no universal law: there is something particularly untheological about a law of priestly celibacy *within the Latin rite*). There are, most certainly, strong grounds for the recognition of the spiritual and practical value of celibacy as a freely chosen state for some who are called to it. Essentially this means members of religious orders, women or men, and the differentiation of 'religious' from the 'secular' or 'diocesan' clergy is one of the most enduring characteristics, and strengths, of Catholic ministry. Yet the value of that differentiation has been eroded by imposing celibacy, a characteristic of religious life, upon the whole priesthood by law and by nothing else than law. There is nothing in scripture, nothing in the early church, nothing in the sound tradition of Catholic theology to justify this law. It grew largely out of a growing but heretical belief that sex was somehow of itself impure and that therefore even sex blessed in the sacrament of marriage was deeply unsuitable for an ordained priest administering the holy things of God. Yet God in Christ took to himself in principle the total *humanum*, all that is not sin. The religion of the Incarnation is not a religion of withdrawal but a religion of holiness within the 'flesh' of humanity. Priests must, in a very special way, represent the balance of Christ's message. If sex is necessarily sinful, then the marriage theology of the Church as it is taught today is nonsense. If it is not sinful but is, indeed, a central if difficult area of human growth and moral striving, then it seems impossible for it to be right that all christian priests opt out – be compelled to opt out – of the totality of marital relations and parental responsibilities.

This means, not only that there is no sound argument against a married clergy, but that there is a decisive positive argument in favour of a married clergy, if the gospel is not to be twisted. The need is particularly pressing in our time. Marriage has always been with us but in the past there was a relatively stable society with agreed moral norms, so that it could appear possible for the clergy to preach about situations fairly effectively even though they were never involved in them. Today this is simply not the case and if priests as a body are outside whole areas of life they can have next to nothing to say about them. Even if Pope Paul is right in his condemnation of all artificial forms of contraception, a clergy which has only to face the issues academically will never be able to convince a doubting laity. If then the clergy are as a whole to remain celibate, the consequence can only be (and is already) an ever growing marginalisation of the priesthood, a disastrous withdrawal into the limited fields of ritual and fund raising.

There is simply no way apart from a married priesthood whereby a clerically controlled Church can credibly demonstrate that it does not still regard the sacrament of marriage as at least one stage removed from the way of perfection. We need married priests not because marriage is easy and celibacy too hard for us, but because marriage is hard and at the same time the normal arena for the practice of christian virtue, including asceticism, while celibacy – unless it be linked with a really vigorous self-discipline all along the line – can easily become, within our affluent society, a way of life with very little moral challenge to it: too heavily compensated for by drink, overseas holidays, hours before the TV set, and a generally rather egotistical pattern of off-duty behaviour, very different from that required of the family man. Of course there are hundreds of priests to whom this just does not apply, but there is too much truth in it for celibacy as such to be a convincing proof of self-sacrifice and dedication.

The moral issue here relates to the whole height and depth of christian spirituality. The point is a very simple one: for as a Christian one is not less wholly at the service of God because one is at the loving service of another human being, but only if one is not serving but dominating. The essence of the religion of Christ (as opposed to every form of gnostic or manichean religiosity) is so to love neighbour – wife, husband, workmates, lepers, the oppressed – that one is indeed loving God and finding God. This central moral insight is immeasurably damaged by a law which compels the whole body of the ordained to opt out from so many relationships which as a consequence are inevitably devalued (as witness the tiny number of canonised saints who were married).

Existentially one can be convinced of this, not only by the lives of so many Catholic laity, including that dearest and wisest of saints, Thomas More, but also by calling to mind holy married priests of other communions. When I hear Pope Paul declare a married priesthood an 'impossible or illusory' solution, I think of Michael Ramsey and so many other married priests of other churches and I wonder what he can possibly mean.

No less important a consideration is that of the position of women in our society. The Church, particularly the post-medieval Church, has continually devalued them, excluding them from all roles of importance. To a large extent secular society did the same and while this did not excuse the Church, it did in some way reduce the pastoral disadvantage of its all male-mindedness. Today with a profound revolution in the social relationship between the sexes in progress, it becomes more and more anomalous and disastrous that the Church be led not just by men only, but by men all of whom have spent their adult lives profoundly segregated from the other sex. It may seem a little thing to female liberationists to argue that at least some of the Church's male ministers should have learnt to understand the female mind through the wear and tear of married life, yet I cannot doubt that the effect upon the Catholic Church would be vast.

I am not arguing that all priests should ideally be married or that celibacy has no value. On the contrary. I disagree profoundly with the Reformation rejection of value in the life of celibacy. It is vital that freedom from marriage be asserted too – a freedom through which it is possible to attain human fulfilment, holiness and great happiness. I even feel that if it were necessary that all priests should be married or all celibate, I would still very reluctantly prefer the latter; but what we must do is to escape from the oppression of this 'either/or' and return to the 'both/and' which did exist in the early church and is called for by any serious understanding of the diversity of gifts in the body and ministry of Christ. Celibacy is immensely valuable in a monastic community, in the missionary life, for shock troops in the Church's struggle against social injustice, and for certain quieter pastoral roles. But the fact that it is so obviously non-normal requires that here if anywhere the freedom of the gospel be strikingly manifest. Its true brilliance is horridly dimmed by the shadow of canon law. As a religious option it bears its own witness even to what marriage is all about – the love which transcends all particular forms. As a general clerical obligation it makes the whole splendid biblical analogy between the marriage of man and woman and the union of God and his people almost ridiculous.

When one challenges the compulsory celibacy of all priests in the western Catholic Church, one is in truth challenging a development of many centuries, and one which relates not only to the Church's attitude towards marriage, women, sex, and the priesthood, but also to the whole stress of Roman institutional polity. One must not be blind to the wider ramifications of this. The law of celibacy is a key expression and condition of a particular kind of Latin clericalism and of the grip within the Church of men over women, of clergy over laity, of Rome over all. It is a matter of power more than of anything else. Outside the context of Roman centralisation it is unlikely that the law of celibacy would ever have been made absolute or been maintained as it stands. Though it precedes the modern phenomenon of Ultramontanism, it is an essential component of Ultramontanism's predecessors, high Gregorianism and the Counter-Reformation spirit. The tide of clerical celibacy flowed in as part and parcel of the tide of Roman domination over the *Catholica,* and if one is utterly convinced that for the sake of the Catholic

Church now more than ever that domination must be decisively challenged and from within, then it would be naive to exclude from that challenge the law of clerical celibacy.

The alternative to Ultramontanism is no less than Catholicity – the joyful recognition that a variety of social and cultural forms are the appropriate body for the realisation of the Spirit of God and the Body of Christ, while the reduction of this to a single Roman model is an oppressive caricature of the proper unity of Catholic Christianity. The liberation and renewal of the priesthood depends upon its diversification and its emphatic liberation from a manichean theoretical substructure. Both are impossible while the law of celibacy remains. The task of reconciling Catholic priesthood with christian marriage is not a giving way to weakness, a concession to worldly times but a challenge to true ministry, to moral endeavour, to prayer and a positive asceticism, above all it must constitute a never too late recognition within the structures of the Church of what the doctrine of the Incarnation is all about – the acceptance of christian truth at its sharpest, of the coming together of word and flesh.

2

A Short History of my
Religious Development

I was born in 1929 in Kuala Lumpur, Malaya, where my
father practised law. I was the fifth child of my parents
and by the time I was two my father had settled his wife
and children back in England though he continued to work
in Malaya until almost the end of his life. The home he
chose was St Werstan's, a large house on the hillside
above Great Malvern in Worcestershire. Malvern had
been his own childhood home and the family had been
established in Worcestershire ever since my great-great-
grandfather, a Rev. James Hastings, bought the presentation of the living of Martley in 1791 with the money of his
wife, a Chipping Norton banker's daughter. It proved a
sound investment. James lived to be a hundred and was
followed as rector of Martley in unbroken succession by
his son, a grandson, a great-grandson, and a great-great-
grandson. The dynasty ruled the parish for 160 years, a

remarkable example of Anglican polity. My cousin John, the last rector in the family, a very gentle old priest and a passionate genealogist, died in 1958, the year I went to Africa. The Anglican side of the family had no further suitable candidate for the living and the presentation was handed over to the bishop – a very proper move but one which we inevitably somewhat regret as the house is very old and fascinating. The Church Commissioners have now sold it, building the present rector a very much smaller and handier home in the back garden.

James had a family of fifteen, the ninth of whom was Charles, my great-grandfather. As a boy he was apprenticed to two apothecaries in Stourport, went on to study medicine in Edinburgh and returned to Worcester to become in time the city's leading doctor, the founder of the British Medical Association and its first president of council until almost the end of his life. Sir Charles was a genial doctor, immensely trusted by his colleagues, a man preoccupied with the public interest – public medicine and the sound ordering of his own profession.

His only son was a lawyer, committed all his life to the same basic line of social reform. He succeeded Lord Brougham as Secretary of the Law Amendment Society. An indefatigable committee man, he helped to found and became the first General Secretary of the National Association for the Promotion of Social Science of which Brougham was chairman. On Brougham's death here too he succeeded him. He had greatly helped his father in the campaign for the Medical Act of 1858, the *Magna Carta* of the medical profession, and was equally interested in the furtherance of popular education and women's rights; he helped sponsor the first women's employment bureau in London and was on the committee behind the establishment of Girton College. In Parliament he chaired the committee on the Police and Sanitary Regulations Bill and pressed vehemently for a married woman's property law.

He was not, however, so attractive a person as his father. While immensely hard working, he was pushing, conceited and somewhat insensitive to the feelings of others, but few people can have done more for the solid advancement of reform in the mid-Victorian age.

My father grew up in this Liberal tradition and took it for granted. He read history and law and had hoped to go later into politics. All this provided one side of our family background. The other side was that of Catholicism. It had entered his own family some time back − a maternal great-aunt became a Catholic sometime in the middle of the century. Dr. Pusey was appealed to for help − but too late. "I did not even know of her doubts, until I heard that she had made up her mind" he wrote to her sister-in-law.

My father's mother became a Catholic in the 1890s, and she was followed by her daughter and younger son. Though my father himself only became a Catholic long after his marriage, he had from that time lived increasingly in a Catholic world. His closest friends at Oxford were Catholics − Francis Blundell of Crosby and Jo Kenyon of Gillingham − so it is not surprising that when he came to marry, just after the first world war, it was to a Catholic and someone, like him, with a Worcestershire background.

My mother's mother, Mabel Hutchison, was a younger daughter of an army officer who had served in India in the Mutiny and finally set off on a private expedition to collect ferns in South America. He caught some strange disease there and died soon after returning. My grandmother had elder sisters who had emigrated to the North West Territories of Canada where they were farming. She went out to join them there, met the Oblate Missionaries among the Indian population and was herself converted. Soon afterwards she married a French Canadian farmer nearby, Charles Michel Daunais, so my mother was born in 1897 as a farmer's daughter on what was still a rather wild west frontier. Her father died when she was three and my grandmother decided to return to Britain with her only child.

Two years later she made a very much more surprising decision – to become a contemplative nun in the Benedictine abbey of Stanbrook in Worcestershire. The Stanbrook Community was founded at Cambrai in the early 17th century by Helen More, a great-great-granddaughter of St Thomas More, and Catherine Gascoigne. In the 19th century it had settled at Stanbrook just a few miles from Worcester, thus reviving the ancient Benedictine tradition of Worcestershire, for if any county can be claimed as Benedictine it is certainly Worcestershire. All its great churches – the Cathedral itself, Pershore, Evesham, Great Malvern – were at one time Benedictine. Just as no county is more quietly English, protected as it was from the full thrust of the Normans by St Wulstan, so none is more Benedictine. Stanbrook must be the largest contemplative community of nuns in Britain and certainly the best known, famous for its singing, its learning, its printing and many other things. Here my grandmother entered while her little daughter was received into the tiny monastic school which existed almost inside the community as many must have done in the middle ages. There she learnt Latin and plainsong and calligraphy, elocution, astronomy and heraldry. It was a strange venture – it is certainly odd never to have seen my grandmother except through Stanbrook's double grille. But it worked well enough; my mother was happy and after some further schooling at Bruges in Belgium and Haywards Heath, she got a job in an Army Pay Office during the first world war and, when it was over, married my father.

A cousin once remarked to my mother that it was a pity one of her three sons could not be brought up an Anglican so that he could carry on the family tradition at Martley, but for us in the 1930s such a suggestion was really just a joke. Ours was a most Catholic household where the parish priest, the saintly Dom Bernard Buggins, could be sure to turn for any help he needed. For the main feast days we would go to Stanbrook; the laws of fasting and abstinence were punctiliously observed, priest guests were made welcome from time to time, while all of us were sent away to Catholic boarding schools. I made my first Communion in the Holy Thorn Chapel at Stanbrook – I well remember the tense feeling that day, so that I nearly fainted before Communion and the very sensible server, a Swiss friend, gave me the water cruet to drink to revive me, thus anticipating the relaxation of the eucharistic fasting regulations by some twenty years. It was at about that time that I decided I would become a priest. My only previous aspirations were to be a herald or an archaeologist. I have really no idea what exactly prompted this decision taken almost as soon as I went to my prep. school, St Richard's, further along the hills at Little Malvern. Never afterwards did I seriously question the fact that this decision had been taken and had to be followed, even when later on at the university I occasionally slightly regretted it.

St Richard's was a very small school run most devoutly and almost too conscientiously by John Keble, a convert relative of the great Keble. The atmosphere was one of profound loyalty to the old tradition. The dormitories were named after More and Fisher, Houghton and Campion; R. H. Benson's *Come Rack, Come Rope* was read to us at night. Here and at home I acquired an almost instinctive sense of continuity both with the old monasteries and with Catholic houses of penal times such as Harvington Hall with all its hiding holes. Little Malvern Church itself had once belonged to a small Benedictine Cell while the Court next door, with its own hiding place, was the home of an old Catholic family, the Beringtons.

From St. Richard's I went on to Douai Abbey School in

Berkshire. By that time we had moved from Malvern to Oxford and our home was a very pleasant flat at 86 Banbury Road. The war was on and it was a convenient place to be while my sisters went to school at Rye St. Anthony. If one side of me has always remained a child of the Malvern Hills, never happier than when walking somewhere between Chase End and the North Hill, on another, my spiritual home became North Oxford, my most cherished pleasures messing around in a punt on the Cher or rubbing a brass in a village church – as at Waterperry where the old vicar told us how T. E. Lawrence had not only rubbed the same brass, but apparently tried to tear it out of the ground. Blackfriars in St. Giles soon became our church of worship and many of the Dominicans our close friends. Apart from them until I left school I can hardly have known a priest who was not a Benedictine. The parish priests at Great and Little Malvern, the chaplain at Stanbrook, old family friends like Benedict Steuart, the monks who taught me at Douai, all were Benedictines. It was the air I breathed, as it was that of my mother and grandmother, and I have always been very grateful that this was so. As a spiritual tradition it combined the liturgy and personal prayer, learning, humanity, humour and an undoubted Englishness. It did perhaps lack urgency and certainly restlessness.

I was fairly happy at Douai. I was a very thin, weak child with flat feet and a considerable fear of my fellows, but Douai was a small protective school and I made a few friends and was on the whole tolerated. I enjoyed theatricals and the debating society. In the former I played the parts of Audrey in *As You Like It*, and Launcelot Gobbo in *The Merchant of Venice*. In the latter I unsuccessfully proposed, against a large Tory majority, the motion that "This House welcomes the victory of the Labour party in the General Election". At the end of my speech on that occasion I quoted the lines from

Chesterton's peom *The Secret People* "We are the people of England and we never have spoken yet" to suggest that now at last the people had spoken. Dom Ignatius Rice, the headmaster, president of the debating society, an old friend of Chesterton's but no friend of the Labour Party, commented gently afterwards that he did not think this would have been G.K.'s view!

My great support and befriender at Douai was one of the only laymen on the staff, Oliver Welch, the History Master, a biographer of Mirabeau. For me history was really the only subject worth studying and Oliver was a wonderful teacher who could fan all my own interests, especially in the constitutional conflicts of the 17th century and the French Revolution. These, rather than any medieval subject, were at that time my chief interest. Barely 16, I found no book more absorbing than Maitland's *Constitutional History* or Thompson's *French Revolution*! But Oliver made me plough through Rousseau's *Social Contract*, Mill's *Essay on Liberty*, and such like. I don't think there was any monk at Douai whom I disliked but there was also no one who exerted any real influence over me – except, perhaps, from a distance the headmaster; but it was a distance and it was only very occasionally that he came nearer to me, as when he found I was reading Aldous Huxley's *Grey Eminence* and arranged for me to discuss it with him when I had finished.

It is perhaps strange, seeing that almost all the priests I had known hitherto were Benedictines, that I never seem to have thought of becoming a Benedictine myself. I saw the monastery as an amiable place but it did not challenge or draw me in the least. My personal religiosity at that time consisted in a particularly critical approach to the religion class, where my queries and objections never ended; in a considerable love for Bishop Challoner's *Garden of the Soul*, a book of devotions which I still prize, and in attending Sunday Vespers, an experience I found very soothing and of value because – unlike most things – it was not compulsory and few boys came.

My heart, however, was now elsewhere, with the young Dominicans I met at home in the holidays – Columba Ryan, Illtud Evans and others. They were regular visitors at tea and companions for outings. Blackfriars had become our spiritual home, a community, it seemed to me, of apostolic vigour, intellectual vitality and many warm and varied characters. I looked forward to joining it.

But first I had to read history at Oxford. It never occurred to me that I would do anything else and fortunately I had no difficulty in being admitted though still very young – I was only 16 when I left school. I went up to Worcester College in October 1946 at a moment when the University was chiefly filled with, to my eyes, rather elderly, ex-service men. I may well have been the youngest boy at Oxford my first term, but I soon picked up a wonderful group of friends whose varied experience was an education in itself.

In my first months at Worcester I was involved in prolonged argumentation with a group of Anglican divines about the claims and counter claims of the Church of England and the Roman Catholic Church. I was particularly out to demolish the arguments of one or two Anglo Catholics whose position I thought then (and to some extent still think) could be pretty preposterous in its acceptance of bits and pieces of high Catholic doctrine and devotion, which did not belong to the Anglican tradition but only made what sense they do inside the (Roman) Catholic system which they reject. I was out to make converts and made none. We argued in good apologetic fashion for a while and then wearied of it. My tutor at that time, old Roberts, a very sound Anglican, would tap his knee with some impatience as I read out my essays with often a good deal of controversial material but all he said afterwards was that I should remember the examiners would be hard-headed people unlikely to be converted by my examination papers! By my second year I had grown a little older and my view of religion less controversialist.

The great influence on my life at this time was that of my new friends, an exciting group of Catholics, mostly converts, almost all of them far older than myself. Several would later become priests and several distinguished scholars. There was Donald Nicholl, John Webb, Robin du Boulay, Mary Tew (later Douglas), Paul Olsen, Robert Murray (later S. J.) Russell Hill (later Edmund, O. P.), Owen Hardwicke and others, as well of course as my sister Cecily up at Somerville at the same time. The sheer excitement of those friendships, the sense of discovery, of belonging to a confident and highly intelligent society, different from Oxford and yet so much at home in Oxford, made of those years one of the high points of my life. We could meet at the 'Gurrin group' in Campion, at a lecture by Victor White or Gervase Mathew in Blackfriars, at an Aquinas Society meeting, after Sunday Mass at the Chaplaincy, or just at tea in our family home in the Banbury Road.

For me the central relationship in all this was with Donald. From a working class Yorkshire background, he had won a Brackenbury scholarship to Balliol, knocked about Asia in the British army, become a Catholic, and was already a gifted medieval scholar and amateur philosopher. His influence upon me was vast; we shared digs in St. John's Street, walked the Yorkshire moors together in the vacations, and went to daily mass and Compline. The affection we had for one another was profound. When Donald was confirmed I was his sponsor, but the true line of influence was all the other way and for a time I almost saw the world through his eyes, but he had soon to leave, to marry and take up a lectureship in Edinburgh. For me Oxford was never quite the same again. Nor was I. I had now read quietly through Dom John

Chapman's *Spiritual Letters* and was regularly studying the New Testament. Maritain and Gilson had become the guides to my wider thinking. I had bought the *Summa Theologica* of St Thomas. I was finding a way forward in prayer and personal study increasingly my own.

I remained deeply shy with the other sex although regular participation in country dancing at the Old Palace did help a lot here. But essentially, and despite some quite considerable regrets, I knew I was committed to the priesthood and believed that this made any real friendship with a girl dangerous and almost wrong, so while my life was full of close male friendships there were no female ones.

This went in part with an ever deepening sense of personal vocation and commitment. I spent much of the summer of 1947 staying in the monastery on Caldey Island and the rigour of the Cistercian (Trappist) life there set me new standards. Hadn't my own ideas of the priesthood hitherto been far too easy going and accommodating? Did not the plan to become a Dominican fit in a lot too comfortably with my own bent and scholarly interests? It seemed to me that I should be willing to offer myself for something a great deal more exacting and unpleasant. At that moment even the life on Caldey, if physically extremely hard, seemed in some ways spiritually agreeable. It was at that moment that I suddenly saw before me a vocation which seemed at the time to be totally unattractive, spiritually or physically, – the life of a missionary in Africa. I was a little Englander, wholly uninterested in the Empire, or in non-European cultures. To banish myself to Africa was a singularly disagreeable thought, but having once entertained it I found it impossible to banish. Over the next year the argument developed. Almost everyone could assure me that missionaries should be strong, practical people while I was as weakly as ever, singularly unpractical and chiefly interested in medieval history. But once I started to read

1. The national cross carrying pilgrimage to Walsingham, July 1948.

This is the Oxford party passing through Letchworth. Russell Hill (now Fr Edmund O.P.) and I are bearing the arms of the cross. Robert Murray is just behind me, Jan Janiurek behind him, and my sister Cecily behind Jan. Our two chaplains the Dominicans Daniel Woolgar and Donald Proudman, are slightly to the right. My brother Peter, leader of this group, is on the far right.

about the African missions chinks of frightening but compulsive light steadily multiplied.

The following summer, July 1948, I took part in the great cross carrying pilgrimage to Walsingham in which 14 groups from different parts of the country spent a fortnight on the Walsingham way. I was one of the Oxford group led by my brother Peter with my sister Cecily as an auxiliary member (women were not officially allowed) and a number of friends. It was a powerful spiritual experience but almost completely exhausted me physically.

The following winter, my last at the University, I realised I had got to make up my mind about the future. I had fought off the call of Africa but it had come back again and again until finally I went down to Douai for a few days over the Epiphany to ask the advice of Dom Ignatius Rice. We talked it over and his first reaction was that I should stay in England but in the course of Mass that feast day he changed his mind: if staying seemed the 'natural' thing to do, going seemed all the clearer to be the way I was called. I took his advice and knew it was final. As I sat in the cold on Didcot station on my way home, waiting for a change of train, I felt as miserable as I have ever done – I had trapped myself, so it seemed to me, on the most depressing of roads. Yet as I look back on it now, no decision do I less regret, no other in my life has proved so fruitful or rewarding. The White Fathers were the only missionary society I knew of, so it was to them I applied. Many of my Oxford friends were going off to be priests – Russell to be a Dominican, Robert a Jesuit, John Day a Cistercian, Michael Griffiths a Benedictine at Ampleforth (and later abbot), several to the diocesan clergy. But I felt that I had become different and rather a loner: I had opted to leave Britain and Europe and I had done it very much on my own. There was not the trace of a missionary movement among the Catholic undergraduates of my time. One evening as I prayed in Blackfriars I had the most powerful sense of the hand of God upon my shoulder. It was more than enough with which to go on.

My last year at Oxford, neverthless, was largely spent on other pursuits, my studies having grown a great deal more mature with the passing of time. They now embraced a considerable concern for trade union history, the 19th century Irish Question and much else, but my two chief areas of interest were early European history and the 13th century. St. Augustine was my way into the former. Jan Janiurek and I had Tom Corbishley, the Master of Campion, as our tutor for Augustine and a very kind and helpful one he was. I went on to study general history from Diocletian to Gregory the Great – a period very few undergraduates took – with C. E. Stevens, the Vice-President of Magdalen. He was a rather famous tutor and, all in all, the best I had though I found it hard to forgive him for losing an essay I wrote on Julian the Apostate. I felt still more at home, however, in the English 13th century and here I was greatly stimulated by the personal interest of Sir Maurice Powicke, a very great medieval historian and previously Regius Professor. Now in retirement he was most kind to a very young student and his became my first real ecumenical friendship. It continued until his death when I was in Africa. Among my heroes at this time was Robert Grosseteste, Bishop of Lincoln. He seemed to me to have achieved a remarkable balance between learning, piety, pastoral action and a wider political concern, but his most intriguing action was his famous refusal near the end of his life to obey the Pope over a matter which he regarded as destructive of souls: 'Filialiter rebello'. Grosseteste firmly believed in the papal authority, as Sir Maurice stressed in a special lecture on the subject, a copy of which he gave me; it was as a Catholic and even as a papalist, someone who profoundly believed in the moral importance of the papal office, that he was finally driven to challenge its abuse.

At much the same time as I was turning over in my mind the lessons of Grosseteste, I was struggling with another point – how much weight could a Catholic properly give to non-infallible papal teaching? We were constantly told of the deep duty of 'docility' in this regard, but what if it were not true, and was not one's primary duty to the truth? I got my teeth into this issue across that little verse in scripture known as the 'Johannine comma'. It is to be found in the Vulgate 1 John 5.7 and refers to 'the three witnesses in heaven the Father, the Word and the Spirit, and these three are one'. It was, of course a splendid Trinitarian text but unfortunately is to be found in not a single early Greek manuscript and is plainly a gloss. The Pontifical Biblical Commission early in the century had declared the verse authentic – one of its many attempts to block the findings of modern scholarship. In this case, however, so clear was the matter that in the 1930s the judgement had been reversed. One was regularly told that the findings of the Biblical Commission were among those which every Catholic should accept with 'docility'. This could only rightly be claimed if they were likely to be true but the case of the Johannine Comma which I had just discovered was enough to settle the matter for me once for all, if it were really so. In the late summer of '48 I was having a holiday with the Dominican Scripture scholar Fr Roland Potter, in Devon, and as we tramped across Dartmoor I hammered out with him all the facts of the case. I was only 19, but it was for me, intellectually, a fairly decisive moment though I did not quite let on. Essentially this was the same sort of teaching as that on Anglican Orders in *Apostolicae Curae* or (later) that on contraception in *Humanae Vitae*. So far as I was concerned it would all henceforth have to stand or fall on its intrinsic merits, not on the decisive claims of papal authority.

I did not, of course, see everything as clearly as that

then or for long afterwards. On the contrary I was carried along to a considerable extent by the high ultramontane tide of those years. My grandmother, Dame Paula, had the greatest devotion to Pope Pius XII and I think we all shared it to a considerable extent. Certainly the White Fathers were highly Roman-minded and it was really only after I got to Rome myself that I started to realise that Rome's position within the Catholic Church was not just something to be defended and lauded as most Catholics tended to imagine.

My last serious work before entering the seminary was to write a twenty page article on St. Benedict's attitude to the hermit's life. I felt that most Benedictine scholars, including the great David Knowles, had somewhat mis-understood this and I still think I was right and my piece was a small but genuine contribution to Benedictine studies. It was published in the *Downside Review* in 1950 just after I had started life in the White Fathers' house at Broome Hall, Surrey, under a régime which was rather like returning to that of one's prep school.

The White Fathers were founded by Cardinal Lavigerie in the 1860s for the evangelisation of Africa. All in all they may well have been the most professional group of missionaries the Catholic Church has ever had. While their origins were strongly French and when I joined them they had never had any one but a Frenchman as Superior General (in 1949 the position was held by a formidable bishop from Upper Volta named Louis Durrieu) they were now a very international society with important provinces in Belgium, Holland, and Canada. The British province, however, was rather small and amateur. I think it can fairly be said that one did not encounter in it – at that time at least – the full glory of the White Father tradition. At Broome Hall no member of the active staff had ever been on the missions nor had any of the teachers the slightest formal qualification to teach. They had inherited the narrowness of the White Fathers' way without much of its experience or vision. I think, quite honestly, one needed a lot of faith to survive two years of 'Philosophy' at Broome Hall, where much of the teaching consisted literally in copying off the blackboard sentence after sentence as the 'professor' wrote it there – but clearly my condition was not that of most of the seminarians. I was the first person to join the White Fathers from an English University, though I was preceded by one from St. Andrew's. Most of my fellow students had no more than some O levels acquired at the White Fathers' own 'minor seminary'. There was next to no library. I was regarded as distinctly odd, if not proud and dangerous, in possessing and reading the *Summa Theologica* and *Contra Gentiles*. Probably I was proud. The culture shock after Oxford was very great and yet I gained a great deal in having to adapt to live with a quite different kind of young man from any I had known hitherto. I was at least dispensed from attending the Church History classes and was even – and very generously – asked to give the course on political ethics, a subject I had worked hard on at Oxford. The fathers did, I believe, really do their best to accommodate me and it was not really their fault if my years with the Society were intellectually an arid time.

From Broome Hall we went to novitiate and theology at S'Heerenberg in Holland where I spent another two years. The novitiate was a time of complete withdrawal and monotony, very long periods of prayer and equally long periods of manual work. There was next to no intellectual fare. It was a time to break one. It did break some and nearly broke me. When many years later I read Solzhenitsyn's *A Day in the life of Ivan Denisovich* it strongly recalled to me the spiritual discipline of the White Fathers' novitiate! Among the minor horrors of that time was a clerical novel called *The Cardinal* which the Novice Master had chosen for reading in the refectory. It

2. At the wedding of my brother Peter in Oxford, April 1950.
My sister Cecily is on the left with Jean and John Webb, Dorothy and Donald Nicholl and myself.

depicted at great length all the stages in an American priest's life until he became a Cardinal – perhaps Spellman was the final model. I found it unutterably third rate, though I believe that quite a number of my fellow novices liked it. For a while I was in charge of the refectory reading, that is to say I had to show each reader where to begin and practise it with him if he was not British. I took advantage of this to jump as many pages of the book as I felt would not be noticed. Even so it went on for many months. Another incredibly dreary book we had for public reading was one of Cardinal Spellman's own travel books; of that I remember remarking to a friend that there was not a single sentence in the book which could not be omitted without advantage to the whole.

What did save one in the novitiate as in 'Philosophy' and indeed, I expect, in almost every seminary was the camaraderie – the very real friendship and sense of common purpose which was built up among us. It made of it essentially a happy time. Nevertheless, if on one side I was being not unsuccessfully socialised into a missionary society with its immense strength, self-confidence and *esprit de corps*, on the other my sense of frustration, my unease not just with the White Fathers but with a far wider clerical outlook they represented was undoubtedly growing. At S'Heerenberg where the Dutch, French and German staff was a good deal better qualified than that of Broome Hall, the sense of the rigid intellectual frontiers within which one was meant to be confined was more pervasive. When I mentioned to a teacher that a book on the Council of Chalcedon, reviewed in the *Downside Review*, looked well worth reading, he remarked coldly that he did not know whether I had special permission to study the works of non-Catholics but he had none. While we were theoretically encouraged to prepare ourselves for our future apostolate by studying the problems of contemporary Africa it was difficult to get far as we were not allowed to read a newspaper – even the *Catholic Herald!* Fortunately press cuttings were exempted from the ban and my family gallantly set about cutting out all the African news from *The Times* and sending it to me. There was really quite a lot of tolerance but one was, clearly, already struggling against the system – the very system one was in the course of being prepared for.

For me by far the most revealing and devastating evidence of what the clerical mind could do at its narrowest came at the end of my very first year at Broome Hall, the summer of 1950. We were camping on the South Coast for a fortnight before going home when one evening I saw that a fellow student was obviously deeply distressed. We went for a walk and he told me of what had happened: he was illegitimate but had never known it. His mother, a very devout Catholic, who greatly loved him, had never dared to mention it. Shortly after his birth she had married, not his father, and had had a large family. Nothing had pleased her more than that her eldest son wished to be a priest. Now, after he had spent a year in the seminary (and several years too in the society's minor seminary), the Father Superior had noticed that the date of his birth preceded that of his parents' marriage and he was to be sent away as no one who was illegitimate could be received into the Society. It was not a decision of the local staff but of the Generalate in Rome. (Of course many religious orders would not have followed such a principle, but would have applied for a dispensation). Naturally his mother was desperately distressed that through her youthful fault her son was losing his chance to be a priest, while for him to discover the truth of his parenthood in such circumstances was singularly cruel. I myself never quite recovered from the effect that this pondered, heartless decision had on my sense of confidence in organised religion.

I spent rather over four years with the White Fathers.

Almost from the start, however, my mind was moving in rather a different direction. It was on the feast of Christ the King – a great missionary feast – my first year at Broome Hall that I suddenly saw that if I wanted to serve the Church in Africa it would be far better to belong to the Church there fully and not to a European missionary society. The White Fathers had accepted the goal of building up a native clergy more genuinely and enthusiastically than almost any other missionary society. At the time there was only one African Catholic bishop, Mgr Joseph Kiwanuka of Masaka, Uganda, and he was certainly the pride of the White Fathers. He had been appointed in 1939 and still no African had joined him among the bishops. Why not? I asked. It soon became clear that one decisive reason was that missionaries did not believe it feasible to work under an African bishop (except for a few very carefully regulated arrangements), hence it was not possible to appoint more black bishops until whole areas could be staffed by black priests on their own. This immediately seemed to me a gravely mistaken policy: the white missionary should rather be anxious to go to Africa as a subordinate to an African superior. So I proposed to offer myself instead as a seminarian to Mgr Kiwanuka and I put this to my spiritual director. He considered it carefully, we discussed it frequently, and I even approached missionaries back from Africa for their advice, but for long everyone was against it. Black priests do not want to mix with white, I was told, they would not accept you and if they did life would be one long martyrdom with such companionship. With such advice it seemed impossible to proceed and I went instead to the novitiate, where I again discussed the matter to the same effect, and so into theology.

As the years went on my own sense of missionary purpose had grown steadily clearer and my own conviction that – at least for myself – I was right. In Theology I was greatly encouraged when I discovered the existence of a small society, the S.A.M., founded by Vincent Lebbe with almost exactly the purpose I had devised for myself. Lebbe was one of the greatest of China missionaries and when the first Chinese bishops were appointed in the 1920s, largely on his instigation, he had seen that they would need auxiliary priests from the West who would simply be at their disposal. So he founded the S.A.M. When one of its members was ordained he was put at the disposal of an Asian bishop and from that moment he had no further commitment to the Society. In the 1950s they were just beginning to think of doing the same in Africa and I wrote and put my case to them. However it proved of no help to me because they had established a firm rule that it was the society, and not the individual, which would decide where its members should go. They mostly went to Asia. I had long made up my mind that I was destined for Africa and they could not accept me under that condition.

In 1953 it became clear that my desire to go to Masaka could not be side-stepped any longer. It was, however, extremely difficult to make a step without active assistance on the part of the White Fathers. Hitherto the Generalate had simply followed the line that I must decide that I had not a White Father vocation before approaching anyone else, but in this case that might well have left me with nothing at all as it was quite uncertain whether Bishop Kiwanuka would be interested in taking on a white seminarian. This position had been taken up firmly by the British Provincial Father Howell, who was really the crucial person and he had presented various (to my mind extremely feeble) arguments why I should abandon my whole plan. At the end of the summer holidays of 1953 I had to go and see him again and I was full of trepidation. I had been at Stanbrook shortly before to see my grandmother where, at that moment, their great and holy Abbess Laurentia McLachlan was dying. After my visit

Dame Paula had gone to see her Abbess for the last time and Lady Laurentia, who had been intensely sympathetic to my plans, asked her how I stood and my grandmother had to say no further forward. A few days later she died and the day after that I saw the provincial. To my amazement he had entirely changed his position, said that he felt I would have to try my special vocation and simply wanted to know how he could help. So we agreed that he would write to Bishop Kiwanuka himself. My family felt that this amazing change which broke the log jam of years in my vocation was the immediate result of Lady Abbess' arrival in heaven!

Bishop Kiwanuka immediately accepted me and arranged that I should complete my theological studies at the College of Propaganda Fide in Rome, so in November 1953 I left S'Heerenberg and took the train for Rome.

I have no regrets at all – and never had any – about leaving the White Fathers, yet I owed them a lot. Several had been extremely kind and helpful to me. They were a highly dedicated and conscientious group of men and I learnt from them in particular the importance of having a clearly thought out missionary strategy and a very disciplined commitment to its implementation. Later in Africa I worked closely with many of them and include many among my friends. The rigidity of their system at that time was doubtless no greater than that of most other societies and in fact in subsequent years no religious order opened up more at the time of the Vatican council than they under their two outstanding Dutch Generals, Leo Volker and Theo van Asten.

When I went to Rome the decision had been *for* Masaka, not *against* the White Fathers, yet the almost immediate sense of liberation after arriving at Propaganda was immense. I had entered a vastly more stimulating atmosphere. I remember how the first morning, when I entered the office of the Rector, Mgr Cenci, I saw at once

3. An audience with Pope Pius XII given to Archbishop Knox and African students from his Delegation, November 1953.

Knox had just been appointed Apostolic Delegate to British East and West Africa. Denis de Jong, now Bishop of Ndola, is next to me. Adrian Ddungu, later my own bishop, is second to the left of the Pope.

on the wall a photograph of Vincent Lebbe, and I knew I had arrived in the right place. It may seem strange that I should have felt so profoundly at home in an Italian run Roman College and one which had had a particularly bad reputation for rigidity. In fact this had quite changed with the coming of Mgr Cenci, a very remarkable and humane man, a Roman of the Romans, poor, wholly unambitious, a priest of great culture and humour, totally given to his job of forming *Propagandisti*. The College had been founded in the early 17th century for the training of secular priests who would be missionaries. It was then in the Piazza di Spagna, and John Henry Newman and Ambrose St. John had lived in it as very privileged members for a while in 1846, and I suppose I was the first Oxford man to go there since them. The seminarists themselves used to be treated with the most severe discipline – there was at one more remote period even a prison in the college for such students as tried to escape! In the 1930s it was transferred to a splendid site on the Janiculum overlooking St. Peter's and after the war Mgr Cenci was appointed Rector and opened up the College in all sorts of ways. Some of the old customs remained without doubt – thus, one's clothes were all removed on arrival and one was clothed instead, from top to toe inside and out in the garb of Propaganda, of which the most important item was an extraordinary black and red cassock with a deep red sash round the waist and various odd fastenings which were quite difficult to do up at first. We were all divided into different 'Cameratas' – groups of students – inside which we normally lived and only in a group of one's Camerata could one as a rule leave the College. In the past the Camerata system must have been very oppressive – one was totally forbidden to speak to a student in another Camerata, even though he was a co-national, perhaps one's brother. And there were terrible legends about such things. In my time, however, it was just a very pleasant international group of 20 people with whom to share one's life; but in the university one talked to whomever one liked and 'recreation' was out of Camerata several times a week.

The Chinese, the Indians and the Australians were the largest national groups in the college in my time, but almost every country of Asia (except the Philippines) was represented, the Africans were growing in number, and there was a handful of Europeans – from Scandinavia and the British Isles, including a thin trickle of English students from Brentwood diocese. We had Maronites and Copts and Syro-Malabaris from South India, and Greeks and even an Icelander. I found it a truly fascinating community, for if most of the students were young with little previous adult background other than a seminary at home, there was, too, quite a scattering of older men, some of them converts.

Mgr Cenci had wisely decided that since it was hard enough to be away from your country physically for so many years, there must be no unnecessary additional mental barrier: so everyone was free to take what newspapers they liked and to order what books they liked too – the college bookshop did a roaring trade, and I was soon taking the London *Observer*.

Then there was the environment. One could visit the sights of Rome endlessly on free days while the Rector arranged wonderful trips to Etruscan tombs and medieval hill towns. The long summer was spent in our villa at Castel Gandolfo, walking in the Alban Hills, swimming, playing games and reading. For some this became a boring time but not for me; I only had two summers to spend there and I enjoyed them immensely. Something of the joy of life I had known in my first year at Oxford I recovered at Propaganda.

This does not mean that everything in Rome was pleasing. Much was, and I was certainly traditional enough a

Catholic to be excited that I was in the Holy City and had spoken to the Pope. The spirit of Propaganda was one of intense Roman loyalty and it took me a little while before a sense of impatience, almost disgust, made itself felt. Many of the students had a passion for attending canonisations and what have you. My mounting dislike for the liturgy of St. Peter's had much to do with my deep-rooted dislike of all complex ritual – particularly all ritual in which I was myself involved. The first time I ever had to serve Mass, – back at my prep school – I made almost every possible mistake and at the supreme moment of the Consecration I had knelt too close to the priest and as he genuflected he kicked me straight off the altar step! I have never appreciated pomp and circumstance, sacred or profane, though I dearly love the lively celebration of liturgical symbols such as the lighting of the Easter candle or the washing of the feet on Maundy Thursday. But the ceremonies of St. Peter's seemed to me almost everything that good liturgy should not be: heavy, worldly, artificial. St. Peter's had, nevertheless, attractions which were difficult to resist: the sheer sense of scale and crowd could be almost overwhelmingly exhilarating on a great occasion but St. Peter's empty was perhaps more deeply moving than St. Peter's full. Led by the Rector, the College would proceed down to the Basilica to say the Creed together at the Confession above the Apostle's tomb. That remains one of the two places in Rome I try always to visit – the other being the monument to Bruno Giordano in the Campo dei Fiori. Bruno, a Franciscan, was burnt to death in 1600. I do not feel it possible to go on identifying with the ecclesiastical institution without also identifying with its victims, the often oddly mixed up people who through the centuries refused to submit to its heavy tyranny: theirs is no less part of the tradition. The Lollards bore the face of Christ at least as much as the bishops. So when I revisit Oxford I like to stand a while in prayer in the Broad with my feet upon that little cross which so unobtrusively marks the spot where Cranmer suffered under Mary.

Rome was in every way large enough for one to be able to love it discriminately. There certainly was plenty to love and to admire. If there was worldliness, even a venality in some of its senior clerics which was frankly scandalous, there were also plenty of senior ecclesiastics who could only be admired. Cenci himself was one of them and another I came to know well was Archbishop Sigismondi, the Secretary of the Congregation of Propaganda, and former Apostolic Delegate to the Belgian Congo. Intelligent, extremely hard working, a little cynical, he lived very simply with his old mother in a flat above his office. He asked me to help him improve his English so I used to visit him there from time to time on his afternoons off and drink a polite cup of tea. For the most part, it seemed to me that if the Curia had a grand front, it had quite a humble behind. The system was highly triumphalistic but most of its servants were no more than devoted, underpaid bureaucrats.

At Propaganda the teaching of theology was hardly an improvement on that of S'Heerenberg. Doubtless our professors were more distinguished but the methods of teaching were execrable and the content was for a great part the most reactionary theology of the time. The die-hard Conservatives of the Council ten years later were well represented at Propaganda! Some were kind enough, such as Garofalo and Visser; others were rather unpleasant and poured out abuse against the German and French theologians whom they accused of ruining the Church. Mgr Parente was not only our Professor of Dogma, he was also the Assessor of the Holy Office – not a fair position from which to carry on personal theological controversy of a very sharp kind. It was not perhaps surprising that he was pushed upstairs and out of Rome – to be Archbishop of Perugia.

I think I did not realise at the time quite what a disastrously narrow theology was being absorbed by many of my Asian and African fellow students who followed the course page by page and nothing more. For me the great relief of Rome was that one really did not need to do this: the student body was big enough for one to be almost anonymous within it and to find one's own way. I learnt rather little from the lectures (partly, doubtless, because I never followed Latin with ease) but I felt free to read as I liked and found myself naturally turning to the writers of the 'Nouvelle Théologie' – Congar, De Lubac and others – so strongly decried by our teachers. I also set about writing once more. Mgr Garofalo had set us off on a mildly personal approach to the Gospels and I found myself more and more fascinated by that of St. Luke. It all began with an attempt to assess the significance of the woman he mentions twice, 'Joanna, the wife of Chusa, Herod's steward'. The study grew wider and wider; from a question of sources it turned into an examination of theological themes, and out of this almost unplanned exploration of the New Testament grew my first real book *Prophet and Witness in Jerusalem*. It was, of course, the work of an amateur; nevertheless its exploration of the meaning of 'Jerusalem' in Luke and Acts is not, I think, without its value, and I am glad that my first book should have been a definitely evangelical one – an attempt to say something about Christ. I am glad too that it began with an interest in a woman – representative of the steadily under-valued side of human and Christian experience.

My interests were not, however, purely theological. At Oxford I had been remarkably little interested in con- temporary issues other than religious ones. But this was no longer the case. It had now become axiomatic that the Church and the missionary task could not be seen apart from a far wider world of modern secular society. I found myself committed not merely to the growth of the Church in Africa but to the defence of African interests and indeed to the defence and interpretation of the non-white point of view elsewhere too. One's friendships at Propaganda seemed to make the espousal of a good many causes natural, if not inevitable, – Goa, Albania, black South Africa. In my first year in Rome I solemnly sat down and wrote a pamphlet outlining the policy Britain should now adopt in Africa; I called it *White Domination or Racial Peace* and Michael Scott's *Africa Bureau* promptly published it. So from then on I could be identified in some sense as a 'political seminarian' or 'political priest' though I have never seen myself quite in that light. Personally I would still judge that I have had rather too little sustained concern with the political than too much, but while I have certainly not served the Kingdom of God with anything of the undeviating selflessness it demands, I do know that the Kingdom of God and not any secular ideal has been the motivation of my various interests.

The experience of Propaganda Fide was one of a 'realised Catholicity'. I certainly did not at that time contrast this with *Romanitas*, on the contrary I took it that the two went together as in the College; to a very real extent, this was a correct view. Rome made it possible for so many national and cultural traditions (doubtless somewhat emasculated but not unrecognisable) to meet and coalesce fraternally *ut fratres in unum.* The College actually stimulated the consciousness of a healthy diversity. I see now that this was to a very large extent the personal achievement of Mgr Cenci – an achievement rather uncharacteristic of the Roman approach – and one that, sad to say, did not outlast his time just as it had hardly preceded it. But for a time it made possible the belief that loyalty to Rome, even as it now is, is fully compatible with a commitment to full-blooded Catholicity. There was much in one's old English Catholic roots, roots which owed nothing to Manning and his followers, to reinforce that belief. Only slowly did it grow on me that the operative Rome was far more of an imperialist, far less of a kindly and creative nurse of the nations than I had imagined. But I have never wholly lost faith in the Rome of Mgr Cenci and I could write some years later of the schism between east and west with full (if almost triumphalistic) sincerity: 'It is for us to show with our deeds that Rome is not as she has seemed: to show that she is already, and will always be, as Greek as she is Latin, a mother to all, for she is simply Catholic. When the Church of Rome really appears Catholic to her critics – the Church of the Indians and the Africans and the Germans and the Americans as well as of the Latins – the old narrow rivalry between Tiber and Bosphorus should die of itself, ... It was the narrowness of national rivalry and the clash of two Mediterranean cultures which caused the schism; it is the breadth of Catholic charity which will end it, when the call of Rome is seen again to be the call of liberty and love and truth!" (*One and Apostolic*, 1963. p. 149).

At Propaganda 'the call of Rome' was indeed 'the call of liberty'. Alas, elsewhere it is too often not so. To expect that anything so institutional would fully respect anything so charismatic is, perhaps, naïve, yet Rome's vocation is to be no less – 'the See of unity' presiding over a fellowship of love made possible by the gospel of freedom. We cannot settle for less, and if at times one has, cost what it may, to say 'No' to Rome, dearest mother of one's own happiest years, mother too of the English Church and of the young churches of the Third World, it is only because the Rome of the Curia is too often not true to itself and its own high calling, beguiled instead by a far less significant ideal of bureaucratic Latinity. The breadth of the Petrine 'See of unity' and the narrowness of the 'Latin Church' are inevitably at war with one another. We fight the one because in youth we were wholly bewitched by the beauty of the other.

I tried even to plot a map of the Catholicity which did not deracinate. *The Church and the Nations* published by Sheed and Ward in 1959 was a direct fruit of the fellowship of Propaganda. Many of the fourteen contributors were found through conversation with my fellow seminarians and one – Tomon of Japan – was at the College himself and a dear friend. It was not wholly successful or as confidently uninhibited in describing the reality of Catholicism in different countries as I had hoped, but it did do something to assert the decisiveness of diversity as well as of unity in the Catholic thing. My own introduction to it (written early in 1958 while teaching for a term at John Fisher School, Purley) was the most mature expression of my thought in the 1950s, but the best thing in the book was undoubtedly the glorious but so little known poem of Chesterton, *Ubi Ecclesia*. Jean de Menasce in Paris had introduced me to it and I resolved to place it at the beginning of the book.

> So abides it dim in the midmost
> The Bridge called Both-and-Neither,
> To the East a wind from the westward,
> To the West a light from the East:
> But the map is not made of man
> That can plot out its place under heaven,
> That is counted and lost and left over
> The largest thing and the least.

But that is to anticipate a little. I was ordained a priest in the College chapel by Cardinal Micara on the feast of St. Thomas, 21 December 1955 with 32 fellow students. Cardinal Micara was Pius XII's Vicar General for the diocese of Rome. He was old and fat and ugly and he must have ordained thousands of priests – a cumbersome ceremony with the repetition over each ordinand of so many formulas. Yet he did it absolutely beautifully and won the hearts of us all, and we had been quite prepared to be highly critical. The day of ordination, when one has been consciously preparing for it for so many years, cannot but be a moment of intense experience – a strange combination of both having arrived and being strangely innocent and pure, symbolically clothed in white. When one's ordination was in Rome, side by side with companions from every continent, engulfed by the infectious enthusiasm of Propaganda, it was not difficult to be carried away with a sense of realised excitement and high commitment to the Church's ministry. My mother and two sisters had come out from England and so had Mgr Val Elwes, the chaplain of Oxford University to assist me at ordination and first mass. He had been Cardinal Hinsley's secretary and always my very good friend, and it was a privilege to have him beside me at those moments – not only a privilege but a practical help, especially at my first mass. My two 'servers' were Emmanuel Wamala and Paul Kalanda, fellow seminarians from Masaka Diocese. One has since been Vicar General, the other Rector of the major seminary. I celebrated that mass very quietly in a little chapel in the College on the altar on which Newman had said his first mass as a Catholic, and I had placed on my ordination card that simple line of Newman which has always meant so much to me: 'Lead kindly light, amid the encircling gloom, lead thou me on.'

My second mass was in the Catacomb of St. Priscilla. It is one of the oldest Christian Catacombs and contains an altar on which clearly the Eucharist has been celebrated since very early times. To go down into the earth and say mass there at the very roots of the Christian tradition was a wonderful experience with which to start one's own priestly life. It was enough. Many priests, ordained in Rome spend their first months saying mass in this church or that, especially of course St. Peter's. I had no desire to do so and felt, for uncertain reasons, uneasy with the

4. Ordination by Cardinal Micara, 21 December 1955.

approach that did.

After saying mass at St. Priscilla I flew home to England with my mother and sisters. What a very privileged young man I was! It was, in fact, the first time I had flown and we needed to do so if we were to be home for Christmas. I had been granted all the necessary indults and so next day we had midnight mass in the dining room of our own home at Childrey. Every member of the family was gathered round the dining room table that night so I was able to begin the exercise of my priesthood not only in some sort of felt continuity with Newman and the earliest Christian Church but in the simple contemporary context of a 'house mass'.

From that time to this the celebration of mass has been the great joy of my life. Right from the start it was, however, a painful joy. Once back in the College, one was now just one among many priests expected to say mass every day but with no one to say it for. Until ordination one was part of the community mass. Ordained, one had to go off to some corner on one's own with a server whom one was perforce withdrawing from the common celebration. Within months I had realised what a very odd and unsatisfactory state of affairs this was and my repugnance with regard to it mounted with the years. I had at that time no alternative to offer, but the sheer sadness of confinement within the privateness of my own mass was very great – particularly so when later I was a member of Bukalasa seminary staff and the community mass was always said by the Rector. At that time it was regarded as somehow wrong not to say mass every day, and, if one did so, it was then wrong even to communicate at another's mass. I remember how a great breakthrough came for me at Christmas midnight mass in 1963. I was a visiting professor of Theology at the University of Lovanium in Kinshasa at the time. It was a daughter university of Louvain and that Christmas the Rector of Louvain was visiting us. He was himself a bishop and he celebrated midnight mass in the immense chapel of the University. Very bravely I went up to receive communion with the laity but I noted that my Belgian priest colleagues did not do so! From my personal viewpoint there is nothing for which I am more grateful to the Vatican Council than the reintroduction of 'concelebration' which has enabled one to escape from the ritual of the 'private mass' which had become in my life by the 1960s quite literally a daily torture. I had, and have, of course, no problem at all with the celebration of mass with no more than a single other person if reasons of time or place call for it.

Fortunately from almost the beginning one could get out at the weekend from Propaganda to do pastoral work in a Roman parish 'without the walls'. I was soon going regularly to a church near Ciampino, so my first sermons were preached and my first confessions heard in Italian. There one could sense oneself already a priest for people, and not just something not far from a sacred object, a dressed up doll.

Essentially the life style of a priest seemed a not uncongenial one. I had been socialised quite effectively into the ranks of the clergy. Celibacy I hardly felt as a problem at all. The remoteness from women which years in a seminary engendered had produced what can honestly be called a case of retarded development. There were, doubtless, bouts of 'temptation' of a pretty immature sort but they did not signify very much and one simply took for granted that the Church's law on the subject must be right. My vocation to the priesthood itself was so over-whelmingly strong that it could have surmounted, almost unquestioningly, still greater hurdles. There was so much profit: a great sense of certainty, of the task allotted, of joyous fellowship with fellow workers, of the worth-whileness of prayer. I believe that many priests found the daily recitation of one's breviary, the Latin 'office', a dreary burden. I did not find it so. Of course it was long – the whole psalter every week and, what was often much less attractive, baroque hymns with difficult constructions, and long lessons containing the lives of the saints, but quite enough of it was a real tool for prayer and something I much preferred to the formal exercise of meditation. It represented, I thought, the Benedictine approach to prayer rather than the Ignatian, which was something I had found uncongenial ever since entering a White Fathers' seminary and discovering their commitment to the Jesuit model of spiritual life. I tried from the beginning, within reason, to say the different parts of the office at the right times of the day and well remember my amused horror when Mgr Cenci admitted that he finished off the recitation of the breviary, including Compline, each morning before breakfast! To say the Church's official night prayers at that time of day seemed to him perfectly reasonable; it seemed to me the height of absurdity.

It was decided that I stay on in Rome to obtain a Doctorate in Theology. At that time Rome was bursting with ecclesiastical students – Pope Pius' policy had been to encourage the world's bishops to send as many future priests as possible to the holy city – so accommodation was becoming quite a problem. I was lodged in a little Italian college called the Apollinare. It held thirty priests presided over by a Rector, Mgr Masi, and a little subrector whose main responsibilities were in the school beneath. The College was intended to cater for Italians studying Canon Law at the Lateran University, but there were now not enough of these so the empty rooms were filled by a couple of Chinese, a stray American and myself. While I liked most of the people I met there, the College itself depressed me exceedingly. Never have I been in a place dominated by more irksome and officious rules. They seemed inspired by a profound lack of confidence, very painful in a house occupied by a small community of priests. No one was ever to be out for supper, even in another clerical college. No visitor, even a priest, could ever come to your room, but had to be entertained in the very dreary little parlour. After every meal we solemnly processed upstairs in a crocodile and there waited for Mgr Masi to pass by and unlock the door of the upper floor where our rooms were. The celebration of daily mass, served by another priest saying his office and anxious for you to finish so that he could take over your vestments and altar while you served him, I found almost traumatic. After some weeks I decided I must try and get away so I appealed to Mgr Duchemin for a room at the Beda. He was most understanding but of course the College was full. If however a student should leave, (which did not happen so often at the Beda) or die, he assured me that I could have his room. One died a week or two later, an elderly man I had never met, and so I was able to transfer to the Beda before Christmas. At the end I felt rather ashamed, abandoning my new friends at the Apollinare in what seemed to me little less than a prison, but when I went to say goodbye to Mgr Masi, he shook his head in a kindly but melancholy way and remarked 'You know the Apollinare has made many popes.'

The Beda had a very different atmosphere. It had its rules – more than legend suggested – but it was very much of a community. It also had better food; it was warm, genial, devout. Not being nearly so close to the centre of the Roman ecclesiastical system, it treated the latter with the profound devotion and superficial cynicism of the outsider, in place of the profound cynicism and surface devotion of the insider. The Beda had been founded for 'late vocations' doing a four year course to ordination instead of six or seven. Its unordained students had to be over 25 and most, I presume, were over 40. Frank Greenan, my kindly room neighbour, was over 70. As to former careers, they included colonels and parsons, teachers, solicitors, doctors, policemen. A fair proportion were university graduates and some very able men; a few had difficulty in mastering the simplest lessons. It would certainly not have been easy to provide a really suitable theological course for such a mixed bag, but essentially no attempt to do so was even made. I was almost more horrified by the courses I found being taught at the Beda than by the regime of the Apollinare. They simply consisted of the standard course taught elsewhere, pressed tight to cover four years in place of six. A great opportunity it seemed to me was being missed at the Beda and the person chiefly responsible was Mgr Duchemin, who had by then been rector for nearly thirty years. No more charming, devout and intelligent Englishman had ever fallen captive to the spell of Rome. This was made possible by his profound anti-intellectualism. He simply did not see the point in theological thought, though he was far too kind and polite ever to suggest that some theologically excitable young priest might be wasting his time. He had for the most part handed over the running of the College to such ex-army officers as he had among the students and no one could be counted on better to ensure a tone of liturgical and theological conservatism.

We were five English student priests enjoying the hospitality of the College while attending a university elsewhere in the city. Though about the youngest members of the community we were treated with great respect and kindness, and I will always cherish the memory of my months at the Beda, listening in the refectory to the reading of Duff Cooper's *Old Men Forget*. (When I stayed at the Beda eight or so years later they were again – or was it still? – reading it!) I soon had the reputation of being something of a radical both in politics and in theology. There was a distinguished Benedictine monk in Rome at that time Dom Gribomont, who was well known for ecumenism and for being sympathetic to the Church of England when such things were not so common. As my thesis concerned Anglican theology it was suggested that I call upon him, which I did one afternoon. We soon got into a discussion about the ecclesiastical situation in England and he soundly berated English Catholics for the narrow-minded lot they are. Naturally I tried to say a word or two in their defence, on which he saw at once that I was one of this short-sighted brood and turned on me too as 'Ultramontane' and 'Post-Tridentine', which I expect in many ways I was, having just learnt my theology in Rome. All the same friends at the Beda were naturally amused that I should have been so described and John Veal, one of the staff, wrote a *Ballade To a Theological Conservative* which began:

Dear Hastings, you're so post-tridentine,
Such a rigid scholastic in hue;
Your theology (far from Cis-Alpine)
Is narrow, Right-Wing and True-Blue.
You're a man who would stamp as non-U
The slightest endeavour to strain
The limited, orthodox view
Of Hastings, the Ultramontane.

I finished off my doctoral thesis the following year while studying for a post-graduate certificate of Education at Cambridge and living at St. Edmund's House, a delightful year in a very sensibly run place which has become for me after many subsequent returns as much a home as I have anywhere. But I will recall one of the less happy memories of those months. At that time no priest was allowed to visit the theatre without episcopal permission. A quite serious, if romantic, historical play, *Catherine*, about Henry V's widow was about to arrive at the Arts Theatre from the Edinburgh Festival and among the cast there was a very old friend of mine, an agnostic. I knew he would expect me to see it and, of course, I wanted to; I was after all, studying how to teach history. So I dutifully wrote to the Bishop of Northampton to ask for permission to go, explaining the reasons. My friend would find it more than difficult to understand my not coming and would only be further prejudiced against the Church. A letter came back to say the reasons were inadequate and permission was refused. I did not go. But in this as in other often comparatively small incidents I was coming to see what a deeply inhuman aspect there was to the system I had, through the priesthood, become tied to. The old bishop of Northampton was not a bad man; on the contrary; he was, I am sure, (though I never met him personally) kindly, devout and hard-working, but all within the boundaries of a highly clericalist view of the Church. I found that I simply did not share that view of the way religion should be. Mgr Cenci often remarked that it was a pity how often when people pursued the Christian virtues they forgot the human ones and when they concentrated on the sacerdotal virtues they forgot the Christian ones. I found that very true. But I was finding too that there was simply a clerical system quite unrelated to any virtues at all, a way of life undergirded with sufficient privileges to compensate for celibacy and conformism, which was increasingly repugnant.

One road of escape from the sense of spiritual confinement the clerical status seemed likely to engender was the life of one's family. I have the impression that many priests get rather little help from this source – perhaps, until too late, they seek for little help from any lay quarter. For me this was not so. My father had died while I was in the White Fathers' novitiate, but my mother and numerous brothers and sisters provided sympathy and informed understanding, financial assistance when I needed it, and hospitality. They were reinforced by other old lay friends especially from the university. It was at least as possible to engage in serious discussion here as in one's clerical circles. The young priest is inevitably under some pressure to fade out of the lay world he formerly belonged to apart from the conventional visit to parents and to become, as regards his personal life, a denizen of an almost purely clerical world. That was certainly the Heenan ideal. Fortunately this did not happen to me and I am most grateful to my family and friends who enabled me to remain more or less normal and relatively little clericalised. They could hardly have done this if they had not shared the same Catholic faith and many of the same ideals and interests. Indeed even my going to Uganda had taken on something of a family enterprise as several members of the family had decided for one reason or another to go there too – in administration and teaching – and even arrived before me.

In the autumn of 1958 I was back in Rome to defend my doctoral thesis on the way to Uganda when Pope Pius died. I had arrived in Africa by the time Pope John was elected. I and my friends had not wanted Roncalli to be chosen. He was known as the Italian and conservative candidate. The man we had hoped for was the Armenian Cardinal, Agagianian, with a splendid beard and oriental dress. He was prefect of the Congregation of *Propaganda Fide* and I went to say goodbye to him before leaving. It was only a day before the Conclave began. Naturally he was very busy and had not found time to see me when he was due to leave for the daily meeting of the Cardinals in the Vatican so he suggested my coming along with him in the car to St. Peters and so I did. It gave us a chance to talk. At that time the newspaper kiosks were thick with pictures of him as highly *papabile* and whenever we stopped at lights people would recognise him and offer encouraging remarks. 'They don't know what they are saying,' he said to me rather sadly. We wanted Agagianian because he wasn't an Italian and appeared so wonderfully different. Of course he was a *Propagandista* as well, and that marshalled our college loyalties. In fact I have little doubt he would have been a dull pope, more Roman than the Italians, too respectful to make any great reforms. Roncalli certainly was the candidate of the Italian conservatives who hoped to block change. I was sadly disappointed when in Uganda I heard the news of his election. How wrong I was, and how mistaken most of his backers were too! He liberated the Church in a truly extraordinary way so that without him I could never be writing this now. For a long time, however, very little of that liberation came my way. I never saw him as Pope and I was not to leave Africa again for over six years.

The diocese of Masaka was one of the most Catholic parts of Africa. The western district of the kingdom of Buganda, situated by Lake Victoria, it straddled the Equator. The earth was good; there was some rain every month; the people lived on bananas and beans and chickens and made their money from coffee. It was a pleasant quiet countryside and I grew very fond of it and of its friendly welcoming people with their fascinating language and rich culture and history. It was not difficult to feel oneself at home. The first day I entered my diocese, I was brought by Fr. Matovu who had been sent by the Vicar General to Kisubi to fetch me. We stopped at one parish for lunch on the way and travelled on unhurriedly. In the late afternoon he brought me to Bishop's House, Kitovu, only to find that the Vicar General was not there, so we moved on to Bukalasa Seminary where he had a room, to find that he was not there either, but was waiting for me at the parish of Villa Maria to which I had been assigned. As we approached Villa we passed crowds of school children on their way home and when we arrived we found that an impressive ceremony of welcome for me with the Vicar General, all the other priests of the parish and some two thousand children had had to be abandoned as I had not arrived in time! While everything had been arranged more than nobly for my reception the Vicar General had forgotten to tell Fr. Matovu where or when to take me. In a way this typifies much of my time in Masaka – great kindness and a sense of appreciation coupled with a constant failure of communication, within a very old-fashioned world ruled by clerics which I tried hard to serve but whose presuppositions came over the years to irritate me more and more.

At that time there were White Fathers on the staff of the two seminaries and White Fathers as chaplains at the Generalate of the Teaching Brothers, the Bannacaroli, at Kiteredde. Otherwise all the priests in the diocese were black as had been the case for twenty years. I had come to join them, proud to be the one white man who belonged to the diocese – 'a white man with a black heart' as Mgr Cenci used laughingly to describe me. So not only my Bishop and Vicar General were black, but so was the parish priest to whom I was curate, the rector of the seminary when later I joined its staff. When I quarrelled with one black man – my parish priest or rector – I could only appeal to another – the Vicar General or Bishop. So it happened more than once and so I had wanted it to be. I found the clergy of Masaka enormously welcoming, very anxious to be understanding, fairly varied in their individual attitudes, most conscientious in their responsibilities. I came to love many of them individually and still do so, and deeply to appreciate their great willingness to accept me into their community. There is certainly no other group of priests in the world I would prefer to belong to even now. I had intended to spend my life with them and if this did not happen I know very well that in part it has been my fault. Since effectively leaving the diocese I have never come to belong to any other group of priests, or even desired to do so. There, amid the low hills and plantations of Buddu County, I felt for a time

I could spend my life. Since that time, I have, as a priest, been at best what Canon Law calls a *'peregrinus'*, if not a *'vagus'* a homeless wanderer, almost a 'hedge priest', something which canonical clericalism distrusts or even abhors.

For the first fifteen months I was a curate, subsequently I was for five years a teacher in the minor seminary of Bukalasa. The central dilemma of those years, though I only saw it clearly in retrospect, was one of giving and receiving. I certainly had not thought enough about the need for receiving, for learning. After all I knew such a lot, I had so many qualifications, I was so much in touch with the great world, I had already written books. I had not realised at all adequately how the logic of my vocation required a profound shift in pace, in attitudes, in priorities, nor how much the people of Masaka could teach me. I tried to be obedient but was so often brought up painfully short when projects I had embarked upon were judged to conflict with custom, with the established order of the diocese and had to be abandoned. Of course my fellow priests were concerned to see whether I really did want to join them, or whether at heart I was simply yet another dominating young white man sure that he had all the answers. Alas, they must often have found me the latter. I deeply regret now that I did not simply relax more on arrival in Africa, setting myself to imbibe its culture, customs, language, unpreoccupied with getting down to *doing* something. Of course the blame for this, such as there is, was not simply mine. The diocese knew my qualifications and certainly wanted to make use of them. The Bishop was extremely anxious to raise the standards in his minor seminary and I was his chosen tool for doing so. It was no surprise then after fifteen months to be moved to Bukalasa and soon to be responsible for almost all the senior English, History and Scripture teaching. From then on I had very little time to study Luganda, visit the villages or learn about African life; for years I had to be, instead, an apostle of the British examination system as applied to the training of priests. In part I regretted this, but I enjoyed it too. I was quite convinced that the training of priests was the most important thing that could be done, and that the African Church needed the best educated priests it could get. So far as in me lay, I was determined to supply them. My health was not too good, so that I never imagined that I could really have carried on for long a ministry of hurrying around the African countryside. If the Bishop wanted me to help educate his priests, I had no doubt that his decision was the right one, though it meant concentrating my time in a field where I was the expert, where I would give rather than receive, and where only too easily, sooner or later, I might be rejected as a dominating and dangerous innovator. What is surprising, perhaps, is how long I lasted, how much support I received and how almost broken I was with misery when the next to inevitable confrontation finally came.

The new African Rector, Father Mukasa, was as anxious as I to raise the academic standards, and largely trusted my judgement over what had to be done, though we frequently differed about the wider régime of rules and prayers suitable for such an institute. He agreed that the curious cassocks the boys still wore in 1960 should be abolished – though many priests in the diocese were loath to see them go – but on many another point we tussled unhappily; I found him restrictive, he found me a 'pusher'. In 1962 we introduced a 'Higher Certificate' (A level) course for which students came also from the minor seminaries of two other dioceses, and while teaching at this level was far more satisfying the strain of reconciling two very different models of education became a great deal more intense. The young men involved were nearly all well over twenty years of age, some of them were intellectually very able and the traditional rules of the seminary seemed to me more and more inappropriate. I was in the awkward position of being a buffer between them and the staff.

The teaching, however, delighted me. I returned to the study of history, (admittedly nearly all English or European history) with gusto and I think that the boys enjoyed it too. Certainly our academic results were excellent. So far as I was concerned nothing but the best was good enough; in comparison with most schools we spent large sums on the library and I doubt very much whether any other minor seminary in Africa could compare with us in this. But here at once I was faced with a problem. Quite a few of the books I felt we needed and that the British Council might even kindly present to us were such as the staff might think unsuitable for any seminarian to see. It might be a picture here or some seemingly dangerous discussion about this subject or that there. It was customary to place all new books in the staff common room to be looked over before entering them in the boys' library. I was librarian and once the books had reached the library they were comparatively safe. I am afraid I developed the system of only setting out the most acceptable books for 'inspection', the others went straight to the boys! One thing I could not bear was the idea of cutting out a picture here or there from some carefully prepared encyclopedia, but I expect it was done on occasion.

One of the greatest joys of those years was the theatre. I threw myself with enormous enthusiasm into the production of plays – *Julius Caesar* in 1961, *Richard II* in 1962 and *Hamlet* in 1963. The enthusiasm was reciprocated by the students and no activity has ever engrossed me more. I remain staggered by the quality of acting and the unfaltering learning of their parts. I don't think I ever had to prompt a single line on the great day, while the sensitive yet forceful playing of Hamlet by John Ssekaggya was a joy that was worth much, – the climax of four years of dramatic progress. The staff appreciated our efforts here

5. With the top class at Bukalasa Seminary, 1961.

and it was not an area in which I ever incurred censorship or criticism. Perhaps the high authority of Shakespeare stood us in good stead!

There was a curious ambiguity in my activities at this time. On the one side I was breaking out more and more from an old fashioned clerical approach to education (to which anyway I myself had never been subjected); on the other, there I was, a minor seminary 'Prof' trying hard to make the system work and being sucked into it all the time. I was certainly more clericalist in my attitudes at that time than at any other before or since. I had accepted the fact that the Catholic Church in Africa needed priests desperately and that the only practical way to get priests of a traditional kind was through more and better minor seminaries, so that for a while all my interests were centred on this struggle. I was never less concerned with theology or the wider problems of mankind than at that time; this does not mean that I had no interest in such things, only that they were in practice drastically subordinated to the task with which I was entrusted and to which almost all my energies were devoted.

As the years went by, however, doubts multiplied. Convinced as I was that the Church needed some highly educated priests, it began to dawn on me that this was just not the right way to provide some sort of regular priestly ministry for the tens of thousands of villages up and down Africa. Even in Masaka where we were far ahead of any other diocese in the whole continent, in the number of our native priests, the prospects were pretty poor. Many other dioceses had not a single native priest and despite the heavy investment of personnel and money in minor seminaries (I reckoned that 10% of all priests in East Africa were now engaged as minor seminary staff) there was little sign of that changing. By 1963 I was starting to believe that the future ministry of the African Church must depend very largely on a quite different kind of priest

– and that one should look instead for less educated men, better adapted to poor rural surroundings, certainly married. Some of the existing catechists would be the obvious choice.

So I came increasingly to question the underlying pre-suppositions of our work. At the same time some of my colleagues were clearly increasingly worried by the liberal tone of my ideas. To talk of the advantages of a married clergy seemed to some a base betrayal of our own life commitment. They began to feel unsure as to whether the Higher Certificate course I was largely directing could be on the right lines, while I was increasingly worried by the illiberal way in which the seminary as a whole seemed to me to be conducted. When the point of breakdown came neither side felt able to compromise. Some very pornographic literature was discovered in the desk of one of the students. The staff felt convinced that there was more of it about, that the whole seminary was being poisoned and that a drastic search must be undertaken at once. I argued desperately that to search the personal possessions of boys in their teens and young men over twenty was an insult to their dignity and would destroy far more priestly vocations than could be saved by eliminating the pornography. Anyone in their senses knew that many of the boys had no intention to go on to the priesthood; they stayed for the education, which was natural in a country where secondary schooling was so limited. They would remove themselves sooner or later and one should not be too worried about their reading. It was to no avail. The whole staff including the lay masters proceeded to search the papers and possessions of the boys quite ruthlessly. I was miserable. I felt that if I participated in any way, any confidence the Higher Certificate students had in me would be wholly lost, so I refused to take any further part in the staff Council and with that – I expect – I forever burned my boats. I find that throughout the clerical world, while much private disagreement can be tolerated, public solidarity is *de rigueur*. To challenge the system is almost unforgiveable. The modern Catholic Church has had no room, at least until very recently, for public discussion, 'opposition' or criticism of authority – at least from priests. To do any of these things is to condemn oneself as disloyal and unreliable. My seminary colleagues, black and white, were following norms of clerical behaviour accepted far beyond our diocese. They were conscientious, kindly men; they simply adhered to a system and to convictions about the way priests should be trained which – at the crunch – I found I rejected, indeed detested. So when I went to England on leave in December 1964 after six years of very hard work the bonds of confidence had been broken, and – though I did not fully realise it – my life vocation lay in ruins. I had wanted to identify with the clergy in Masaka diocese cost what it might. I had been told in advance that it would be too hard and I had not believed it, and I was right not to do so. What I had found too hard was not that they were black but that – as it seemed to me – they had inherited standards of a closed-in clericalism which as I grew older I found more and more impossible to share.

After a year in England I returned to Africa at the end of 1965 to what was to prove, wholly unexpectedly, an astonishingly different kind of existence. The Vatican Council had been in progress for four years and was now over. One of the causes of personal frustration in my life was that I had had absolutely nothing to do with the Council, indeed through all the years at Bukalasa I had been far too busy to keep up adequately with serious theological work of any kind. While I had hoped that sooner or later I might be transferred to the staff of the senior seminary to teach theology or be offered a university post (I did have two exciting months as Visiting Professor of Theology at the University of Lovanium,

Leopoldville, November 1963 – January 1964), it was
clear that there was great if concealed opposition to any
such move: I was marked already as dangerous – quite
why I never knew, though I suspected it was particularly
connected with my championing (albeit discreetly) the
cause of a married clergy. Anyway while hundreds of
Catholic theologians, some of them of no great distinction,
had been nominated *'periti'* for the Council, and many
more had been asked to advise their bishops, read over
draft texts of decrees and so forth, I had never once been
asked to do anything whatsoever. I had never seen the
draft of a single decree nor put one foot in Rome while the
Council was on. I did not expect to be asked to do much
but it was frustrating to be so wholly left out when such
great events were happening.

But now it was over and for a while the windows were
open and theologians were actually wanted. For a
theologian it was a sort of bliss to be alive in those years
after the heavy suspicions of preceding decades, and I,
most unexpectedly, was suddenly to be offered a share in
it. It did not look like that when I arrived back in Masaka
in December 1965 and was assigned as a curate to one of
the most remote parishes of the diocese. It seemed a
strange appointment but it proved a very happy one. I
loved Bigada and soon developed a relationship of the
most complete confidence with the parish priest, Mgr
Kukera and his septuagenarian assistant, Petro Kibula,
who welcomed me most generously. To be visiting outly-
ing villages to say mass there once more, Ssanje and
Mayanja and Katunga, to be preaching again in my bad
but fairly flowing Luganda, to be hearing Confessions in
Mutucula prison (where a few years later one of Amin's
first ghastly massacres would take place), to be running
out to put my buckets beneath the roof gables when it
rained – all this was somehow very satisfying and
worthwhile. There was obviously so much to do, though

the return in particularly bad form of the malaria which had plagued me in the past quickly made it clear that my life at Bigada could only be a short one.

It proved to be very short. A group of East African bishops led by Bishop Blomjous of Mwanza were planning a programme to put the Vatican Council across to the dioceses of East Africa. It was only too clear that hitherto hardly a hint of what the Council was all about had reached these countries. And though the bishops themselves had diligently attended all four sessions it was fairly clear that the grasp most of them had of the subject was somewhat slight. A theologian must be found and somehow or other he must explain it all! But where in Africa was there an unemployed theologian? At that point in the discussion someone kindly suggested me: just back from leave, probably available. My bishop, Adrian Ddungu, was at once approached and proved delighted to let me go. He had been somewhat embarrassed as to what to do with me. A real personal friend he wished me nothing but well, yet in his very conservative diocese I was now regarded as a dangerous revolutionary. This did not mean that much affection for me did not remain among the clergy. It most certainly did but the gap in attitudes and the suspicions this engendered made it almost impossible for me to be employed in any sort of work for which I was reasonably suited. So when A.M.E.C.E.A. (the joint board of bishops) asked for me and I wished to go, Bishop Ddungu was naturally happy to give the project his blessing. I am glad that I did not leave Masaka on my own impulse, nor because I was pushed, but because the bishops of East Africa asked that I be seconded for what was to prove two years of very hard work based on the seminary of Kipalapala in Central Tanzania.

At Kipalapala there was a fine printing press beside the seminary whose rector was at that time the extremely charming and capable White Father, Theo van Asten, soon to be elected General of his Society. The plan was to produce twice a month an eight page explanation of some part of the Vatican documents which would be printed and dispatched in bundles to every one of the seventy or so dioceses of Kenya, Malawi, Tanzania, Uganda and Zambia. The point of the explanation was to be as pastoral as possible – to help the busy clergy of these countries to apply Vatican II in their own work, and in two years to work through all the sixteen constitutions, decrees and declarations of the Council. The original plan was that I should have two assistants and that all I wrote should be vetted by the seminary staffs. Both provisions proved impracticable. The two assistants never materialised, the seminary staffs were too busy or simply declined to cooperate – though Theo always read through whatever I asked him to. But it was to be I alone, or nothing at all, and A.M.E.C.E.A. was soon delighted to find my commentaries pouring out – all anonymously – as they had decided that my name must nowhere appear. This proved a good thing as it really increased the authority of the bulletin. One good archbishop who did not know quite what had happened wrote to thank the A.M.E.C.E.A. secretariat in Nairobi for the bulletin but suggested that each separate sector should have the name of its particular author underneath it. We sent out some 5000 copies of each number and never, I am sure, have I done more solidly useful work.

It was certainly a challenge. I had had no experience of the Council and effectively no one to turn to who had. All I did have was the complete collection of the drafts prepared for each decree, lent me by Archbishop Mihayo of Tabora. It was fascinating to work from them and a most worth while theological re-education for myself. Of course, the value of my commentaries varied and I probably missed some points which should have been stressed.

Nevertheless the work met a great need at that moment, and not only at that moment, because as soon as it was finished John Todd republished it in Britain as a two volumed commentary on the Council and it continues to sell. I think I am right in saying that there is no comparable work in English covering all the documents of the Council, seriously but briefly, and I may be the only person in the world who has had the temerity to comment on all sixteen documents. In defence I can at least urge that I did it under episcopal instructions! I was immensely grateful for the confidence this did, despite everything, demonstrate, and I am sure the restrained balance with which I tried to approach question after question demonstrates as well as anything how much more likely the bishops are to be well served when they trust than when they distrust.

The two years at Kipalapala were followed by an eighteen month assignment to Mindolo Ecumenical Foundation, also under the aegis of A.M.E.C.E.A. Mindolo is a large interdenominational social training centre on the copperbelt in Zambia which had been going for ten years when I joined its staff as 'Resident Roman Catholic' and 'consultant theologian' in 1968. Hitherto it had developed without any formal Catholic cooperation. The bishops in Zambia were anxious that this should now change and arranged that I should go there 'to break the ice' – though there did not prove to be much ice to break. At the same time I was to be available, as I had been while at Kipalapala, for diocesan seminars and the like, all linked with the post-Conciliar renewal programme. This meant that I visited a good many dioceses for quite intense sessions of two or three days. As a consequence my knowledge of Africa grew apace, as I discussed in place after place the problems the clergy were facing – problems of ecumenism and religious life, of new religious movements and independent Churches, of marriage, of liturgy, but above all, of the organisation of the ministry and the shortage of priests. The more I saw the more convinced I became that despite the immense growth and vitality of the Church or perhaps just because of them, it was set upon a course of disaster on account of the rigid canonical structures, of the priesthood and of marriage, which were steadily strangling the life of the Church in Africa just as had so long been the case in Latin America. Eighty per cent of priests were foreigners and at any time might be compelled to leave; moreover missionary vocations in Europe and North America were falling fast. It was madness not to look for alternative forms of priestly ministry. I found that more and more priests agreed with me, and bishops too, but that the nuncios were trying hard, on explicit instructions from Rome, to silence the discussion. What I saw as my especial task was the elucidation of the structural issues involved in Church growth outside Europe and Europe's white colonies. In century after century, in Latin America, Asia and Africa the Catholic Church – despite the heroism of many missionaries and much good work – had manifestly failed to clear the hurdle, and the basic fault lay in the heavy unadapted clerical structures of the Latin Church. The Vatican Council had repeatedly opted for pluralism within the Church, but in structural terms had failed to draw the necessary conclusions and my work in those years was done in deepest loyalty to the major guide lines of the Conciliar documents. Perhaps the message I was trying to put across was expressed as clearly as anywhere in a key passage at the heart of my *Church and Mission in Modern Africa* (p. 187), written in 1966 and published the following year:

> 'To save the Church in Africa today we have, more than anything else to declericalise her. We have to declericalise the liturgy: to make it again a genuine common action, a parish communion, not a

Latin ritual, performed silently and unintelligibly by the clergy. We have to declericalise Scripture: caring that it is read not only by priests in their breviaries, but to the people and even by them in their homes. We have to declericalise parish organisations, giving real responsibility for the Church of God to all the members of the people of God in the area. We have to declericalise the apostolate, making the layman realise that the mission to bear the light of Christ to convince the world, belongs equally to every baptised and confirmed child of God. We have to declericalise marriage, recognising it again as essentially a human contract between two people to be manifested according to the customs of human society. Finally, and most difficult of all, we have to declericalise the ministry.'

I wrote those words probably at Bigada. There we had some eight thousand Catholics in the parish and about fifteen chapels besides the main Church. Ssanje and Mayanja had a good thousand Catholics each and could well do with a full time priest but there was absolutely no likelihood of their receiving one. If they had mass every month they were lucky. Our furthest chapel, Katunga, was twenty-two miles away on poor roads, so in size our parish was a great deal smaller than most in Africa. To serve it there were at that time three priests: Mgr Kukera, the parish priest, was sixty. He was assisted by Fr Kibula who was well over seventy and one young man, Fr Kyenkaga, who was far from strong and often absent. I was a fourth, wholly extra. Kukera had a motor cycle, Kibula a bicycle which he now hardly used, Kyenkaga a dilapidated car frequently out of order. The smaller churches were fortunate if they were visited by a priest twice a year. The parish had very little money and Kukera wisely spent a fair part of his time looking after the vegetable garden. Kibula taught some religion in the primary schools next to the church and heard confessions but he seldom moved out of the compound. What was clear as day to me at Bigada was that the African clergy were being expected to do an impossible task. Mgr Kukera was an excellent parish priest, a person in whom I had the most absolute confidence, but the work was beyond him. Yet there was simply no relief in sight. On the contrary. In other dioceses distances were far greater (outstations being even a hundred miles away from the main parish), the number of African priests far fewer. When I visited Benin in Nigeria in 1972 I saw in cathedral house a large chart drawn up by a missionary listing over fifty places which the cathedral clergy should be visiting. At that moment the cathedral clergy consisted of just one Nigerian priest asssisted on Sundays by the aged bishop.

When in seminar after seminar I pointed out that this was just not viable, I was often regarded as a pessimist. Attempting to predict the future I suggested that while the number of priests would indeed increase, the number of the faithful would do so a great deal faster for a long while to come and that the consequence would be an ever greater disintegration of the Church as a pastoral institution. I was partially wrong in this, for statistics today indicate that I was not nearly pessimistic enough. The total number of priests at work in Africa has actually been falling year by year in the 1970s. It is true that there are considerably more African ordinations than there used to be but they are insufficient to offset the increasingly rapid decline in foreign missionaries. So while the number of Catholics in Africa has almost doubled since I wrote *Church and Mission in Modern Africa* in 1966, the number of priests is no more at all – and even then they were impossibly few for the task.

Karl Rahner has stated it as an axiom that 'If the Church in a concrete situation cannot find a sufficient number of priestly congregational leaders who are bound by celibacy, it is obvious and requires no further theological discussion that the obligation of celibacy must not be imposed' (*The Shape of the Church to Come*, SPCK, 1974). That has been obvious to me all these years, yet Rome has steadily blocked every realistic proposal to save the African church from what is already a vast breakdown of the Catholic ministry and sacramental community, a breakdown largely hidden from the world by ignorance and by the bombast of church leaders. I don't know how many hours I spent working over these issues on my own, agonising over them, writing about them, speaking in country after country. Even after returning to Britain in 1970 I was invited for hectic lecture tours in South Africa in 1971, Nigeria in 1972 and Rhodesia in 1973 which were mostly devoted to discussing what I called 'the three Ms' of Mission – ministry, marriage and money. In Nigeria I gave fifty lectures of roughly two hours each (including questions) in twenty-eight days, a week each in Ibadan, Benin, Akure and Jos. While I found that the amount of agreement obtainable in such seminars from realistic priests and nuns was remarkable, I have often wondered whether the net effect was not counter-productive to the end I had in mind: the more clearly the need for systematic change in the ministry was spelt out and the greater the necessity to separate the ordained priesthood from a certain type of clerical status, the more determined those in authority appeared to be to dig their ostrich heads into the sand.

Privately many African bishops agreed that with the present system there was precious little hope for their dioceses when, in another decade or two, the foreign missionaries faded away. But they were insistent too that they could do little about it: on the one hand the *fiat* of Rome was too precise, on the other it could seem to the discredit of Africa if its bishops were the first to press for a married clergy when all the other continents had apparently adhered to the high standards of celibacy! Understandably the new bishops of Africa, with a few exceptions, had not the self-confidence to challenge the universal church over this vital issue. It then became clear to me that even if the need was most acute in the third world, the battle for a change of law could only be won in the first world. It was no good endeavouring to make of Africa (or Latin America either) a special case. The younger churches of the southern hemisphere could only be saved if the Universal Church ceased to strangle them with its misplaced regulations.

At the same time I had come to the conclusion that for other reasons too it was time to leave Africa. I could give the impression of lecturing the African bishops. There is no reason why bishops should not be lectured but they were mostly new to the job and had got to be left space to make their own decisions. I did not want them to be bullied by Rome but then there was no reason why they should be bullied by a white intellectual either. I had made my point clearly enough and by 1970 I felt that I no longer had a clear position within the African Church and could best withdraw to England. There was certainly no great desire to employ me any longer out there, perhaps for obvious reasons. I saw my own withdrawal both as a natural step within the Africanisation of the church which I had called for as much as anyone, and as an aspect in what one may well describe as the post-*Humanae Vitae* state of the Catholic Church generally. *Humanae Vitae* in 1968 had proved a watershed, even if some of its implications took time to come through. Certainly the brief alliance of bishops and theologians, which had characterised the Council and immediate post-conciliar years, was over and instead one was back to a condition of distrust. It was not, of course, merely a matter of contraception (though I made my non-acceptance of the encyclical's teaching quite clear) but of a growing range of issues which separated one from the current stand of the *magisterium* and could make it more and more awkward to be employed in theological teaching and planning.

This was not, nevertheless, the only or even the most immediately decisive reason for leaving Africa. Health was another and quite sufficient. By 1970 I was getting an attack of malaria almost every six weeks. No prophylactic had ever succeeded in preventing this and the effect was depressingly weakening; there just did not seem to be any point in going on when so far as I could see whatever work I was suited to do had now been done, and nobody much wanted me anyway. So when my period at Mindolo Ecumenical Foundation came to an end early in 1970 I packed my books and returned to England. Some of them were still at Bukalasa where they had remained since I left in 1964, others were at Kipalapala. I sorted them out, gave about half of them to seminary libraries, and the other half came back to Britain by boat with my mother who had been my housekeeper and companion at Mindolo, just as she had earlier shared my work in Uganda by teaching English in the seminary at Bukalasa. She was now well into her seventies and glad to be getting back to Europe, but she has never ceased to be a rock of love and understanding.

The place where my books are represents home for me, so this was a fateful moment – the intentional reversal of a decision to go to Africa for good taken in principle more than twenty years earlier. Time had moved on, the world and the Church had changed, and I had changed with them. My vocation to be a priest had in its final form seemed inseparably bound with the idea of identifying myself with black clergy. If just before ordination this had suddenly proved impossible, I really do not know what I would have done. But now it *had* proved impossible, or at least to my perhaps more middle-aged eyes no longer practicable, and with it any clear external shape for my priesthood and clerical status had more or less disappeared too. I still love, and am even homesick for, Masaka diocese, the grass thatched village churches and banana plantations of Buddu; and I feel intensely distressed for the sufferings of the people of Uganda under the senseless tyranny of Amin – my old rector, Fr Mukasa, was dragged out of church and murdered by the soldiers, only one of thousands of innocent victims. Yet I have no doubt that I was right in deciding to find a different way. I wrote to St. Edmund's House and asked for a room and wondered what should come next.

What did come next was a wonderful offer of work from the Anglican communion. For years my relationship with Anglicans had been a major part of my life. The Church of England had always been something very close: the God-given sparring partner to be argued with, laughed at, learnt from, loved. An English christian cannot really get away from the Church of England, certainly not an English christian with a strong Anglican family background, and Oxford education and an interest in scriptural and patristic scholarship. I was making Anglican clerical friendships already as a seminarian in Rome. When it came to choosing a topic for my doctoral thesis I settled on that of modern Anglican ecclesiology and while I certainly wanted to try and show why it was wrong and ours right, I felt from the start that this would have to be done not in the terms of government and papal primacy which Catholic apologetic had so much centred on but in those of the necessary unity of ecclesiastical society as such. Little by little, with help from Catholic theologians like Congar and De Lubac but also from Anglican theologians such as Gregory Dix and Eric Mascall, I discovered for myself the theology of 'communion' which is (I have ever since been convinced) by far the most satisfactory word upon which to centre an account of what the Church both is and should be. It is not, as such, a jurisdictional word but a sacramental one and it relates the Church integrally to its central sacrament: the Eucharist. The profound relationship between Church and Eucharist – each truly a 'communion', each 'the body of Christ', one 'the People of God', the other the Covenant whereby it becomes so – has ever since been the hinging principle of my ecclesiology. This principle has proved over the years to be open to a growing flexibility of application which has not dulled but rather intensified, the basic vision. Far from separating one from Anglicans and other christians, this rediscovery of the ancient Catholic conception of the Church brought one vastly nearer to them. A theology of communion was later to be basic to the documents of Vatican II, especially to the Decree on Ecumenism. I was very fortunate to get my ecclesiastical sights right on this point from the start.

Early in my time in Uganda I was able to make friendly contact with John Poulton, at that time Warden of Bishop Tucker College, Mukono. Relations between Catholics and Anglicans had not been good in Uganda and the informal theological discussion group which was already formed before the Council, with the help of my dear friend Joop Geerdes, the White Father editor of the *African Ecclesiastical Review,* was certainly something of a breakthrough. Personally I had a lot to learn about Anglicans – the more one knows of another church, the more there is to know – but contacts multiplied and little by little I have learnt a very great deal. The most exciting moment, perhaps, was one day in 1966 when as I was busy at Kipalapala working away on my *Post-Vatican II* bulletin I received a letter from Mgr Willebrands. It was to ask if I would be willing to serve as a member of the International Anglican-Roman Catholic Preparatory Commission which was being prepared in consequence of Archbishop Ramsey's historic visit to Pope Paul in April of that year. I had never been on any such body or in any

6. The Anglican-Roman Catholic Joint Preparatory Commission, final meeting at Malta, 1 January 1968.
Left to right: Front row: Bishops Gomes, Knapp-Fisher, Butler, Helmsing, Moorman, McAdoo, Willebrands, de Soysa and Fox. Middle row: John Satterthwaite, James Atkinson, George Tavard, Michael Richards, John Findlow, the author, Camillus Hay and Louis Bouyer. Back row: Eugene Fairweather, John Keating, Eric Kemp, Albert Mollegen, William Purdy, Howard Root and Massey Shepherd.

way in touch with the Secretariat of Unity so this invitation was not only wholly unexpected (I still have no idea who suggested my name to this quite small and select body) but immensely heartening. The three meetings of the commission in 1967 at Gazzada, Huntercombe and Malta proved in some ways a turning point in my life – they brought me into the high world of international theology where I soon felt that I could well hold my own, and they crystallised in me something of a sense of mission in regard to the Anglican Communion.

Hitherto my attitude here had been decidedly ambiguous. At the personal level I now had many Anglican friends; at the intellectual level I had continued to do a great deal less than justice to the central Anglican positions. In the 1950s, when writing my thesis, I had been fairly well in advance of the main Catholic line and had even risked getting shot in the back when I criticised, in print, the received Catholic position on both Anglican baptism and ordination. But, basically, I still 'unchurched' the Church of England in a pretty simple way while during the years of the Council I had been too cut off from current thinking and too busy school teaching to rethink my own position very substantially. The Joint Commission forced me to do this and to come to realise that the 'sharing in communion' which constituted the Catholic and Christian Church is a far more subtle matter than I used to think; that any sharp cutting off at the borders of the Roman communion, as today constituted, would be a nonsensical denial of the realities of faith, grace and sacrament, and such a cutting off would seem to savour of the very juridical ecclesiology which I had in principle rejected years earlier.

From 1967 on I felt almost as much committed to the cause of reconciling Anglican and Catholic communions as to the task of transforming a 'mission church' in Africa into a self-ministering, self-governing, self-supporting one.

The next year I was invited by Trevor Huddleston, then bishop of Masasi, and the two Catholic bishops in the same south-eastern corner of Tanzania, to advise them on how to further the quite exceptional degree of cooperation and indeed integration which was developing between the two churches there. Later that year I moved to Mindolo Ecumenical Foundation and my ecumenical activities grew more and more central to my life. I was becoming convinced by this time that the full reunion of churches is indeed a possibility in our time, if we do but work hard enough for it, and that I at least would not be forgiven if I spared any effort in this endeavour. However, I was realising too that reunion would depend less on the presently unattainable formal agreement between authorities or even on the acceptance of some particular model of the Church, but more on an anarchic growth into an inextricable sense of being one and behaving as one. I felt, and feel, quite sure that the essentials of Catholic order would well survive such a process. At the time of the Reformation the real schism did not come at some precise moment prior to which there was full unity, but came after a relatively lengthy breakdown of ecclesial confidence and sacramental sharing and for years afterwards there had been many bonds surviving despite the fiercest condemnations. I began to believe that the only feasible way of restoring unity was a similar process but in reverse, and I found myself committed to being someone who would help to remake the one Church by simply behaving, so far as I could, as if there was but one Church now.

One of the last things I did in Africa in 1970 before leaving Mindolo and returning to Britain was to preach the annual retreat to the Anglican clergy of Zambia at the invitation of Archbishop Oliver Green-Wilkinson. I talked to them at length about the Mass as the centre of the Church: I could not really have agreed to preach such a retreat to priests without speaking about the significance of their central sacramental ministry and, equally, by doing so I was saying something very important about their Church, and I was saying it to myself as well as to them. On my way home I had a further request from the archbishop who had become a dear friend. Could I undertake a survey of the whole issue of the relationship in Africa between customary marriage and church marriage, a survey to be sponsored by all the Anglican archbishops of Africa? So just at the moment that I found myself without a job from the Catholic side and no suggestion as to what I could usefully do, the Anglican Communion sprang forward (somewhat unaware of how opportune it was from my point of view) to propose this fascinating study. There were difficulties, of course, because I was determined to clear it fully with the Catholic authorities and because in the meanwhile Archbishop Oliver was killed in a car crash. However his successor Donald Arden was equally enthusiastic and supportive and the result was that for the next two years I was in the full time employment of the Anglican Communion.

I learnt a great deal from the preparation of the report *Christian Marriage in Africa* – about marriage, on the one hand, and about the Anglican Communion, on the other. It is perhaps the only time that an official report of one church has been written by a member of another. I immensely appreciated the confidence this demonstrated and I tried hard to see things from a sufficiently Anglican point of view while contributing the sort of additional insight which could be expected from someone within the Catholic communion. To stay with Anglican bishops and priests up and down the continent, to discuss marriage issues with little groups of clergy, laity, theological students, to endeavour to obtain an overall view of the situation in nine very different countries and to relate that to theological principle and the limited possibilities of pastoral strategy was an intensely interesting and challenging experience. It forced me to think very hard about the nature of marriage, the Christian attitude to monogamy and polygamy, and the history of marriage as a legally recognised state.

I finished off writing the report during a term spent happily as a visiting lecturer at Lincoln Theological College in the early summer of 1972. There was still no sign of any interest in employing me on the part of the Catholic Church so I was rather relieved when Bishop Shevill of the United Society for the Propagation of the Gospel, one of the two main Anglican missionary societies, suggested my joining the staff of their College of the Ascension on the ecumenical campus of Selly Oak in Birmingham as a tutor. This prolonged my employment by the Anglican Communion for another year and a half, and I must record the sensitivity of that communion and the apparent ease with which Anglican bodies managed to accommodate a 'Roman' (as they would too often, to my continued irritation, mistakenly describe me) in their midst. Participation in the training programmes of Anglican priests, many of them married, at both Lincoln and Selly Oak was of considerable value to me personally; it certainly provided the opportunity to obtain a more concrete sense of the strengths and weaknesses inherent in a married clergy. I could not fail to see that a number of the marriages I observed did not have the strength and sense of thought-out purpose needed to support the ministry of the husband. In some cases, I have no doubt, this was largely because the latter had himself no sufficiently clear idea of why he had become a priest anyway, so his wife could hardly be expected to share it. At the same time I have seen some Anglican clerical marriages of splendid strength and joy. It would be foolish to imagine that a mere decision to allow Catholic priests to marry would solve all our problems, and it would undoubtedly create some quite serious new ones, especially in the short run.

But it would be equally foolish to imagine that the experience of other communions provides any sort of argument against the viability or spiritual seriousness of a married clergy as such.

While at Selly Oak I was happily able to take a regular part in the ministry of the Catholic university chaplaincy of Birmingham. Fr Rock's hospitality here was much appreciated and so was the liturgical atmosphere at Newman House. It was interesting to pass on a Sunday, as I often would, from the Eucharist at the College of the Ascension to that at the Catholic chaplaincy. I have to say that I preferred the latter. The cup was always given to the laity in both places but there was, I think, a rather greater sense of flexibility and warmth in the Catholic Mass. One reason for this, which I find important, was the giving of communion to fairly small children as is normal in the Catholic Church. There are few things I think more misguided in the Church of England than the exclusion of children from communion until after confirmation, conferred when they are in their mid-teens. The order Baptism-Confirmation-Communion is undoubtedly the traditional one and the Anglican Communion in this as in so many other things is materially more traditional than the Catholic. But I have no doubt that we should be very grateful to Pius X for establishing the right of quite small children to receive the body of Christ (and now, hopefully, the blood of Christ), and I hope myself that we go even further in this direction. It seems natural to me, especially in a house mass, to give communion even to the smallest present. The understanding they have is that appropriate to their age, and that is enough for God. The alternative is an act of exclusion which seems quite wrong and may well be far more painful than we realise.

Many of the things I argue for such as communion of the cup, a married clergy and the election of bishops are commonplace in other churches and Catholics at times

7. In my office at the College of the Ascension, Birmingham, July 1973 (by courtesy of the *Birmingham Post*).

accuse me of foolishly imagining that 'the grass is greener' over the wall and even of wanting to cross the wall. Such is not the case. While it is true that these are practices in some other churches and Catholics would be unwise not to learn from them when appropriate, in fact they are integral elements in the very best Catholic tradition. In accepting them we would be true to ourselves – to the width of a wide catholicity rather than the narrowness of a closed post-Tridentine one. It is far more the intrinsic requirements of our own historic continuity, the very formulas of our own liturgy, than an imitation of the practice of any other church which have been decisive for me personally. I asked a charming Sacred Heart nun who spent a year at Selly Oak while I was there what she had gained from it. She answered that she had come to Selly Oak a Protestant but would leave it a Catholic. That was a profound remark but I expect that many people who have had ecumenical experience would feel something similar. The first tendency may be one away from one's own tradition in the excitement of discovering so many good things elsewhere. Subsequently, however, while assimilating some of those things into oneself and one's own spirituality, one is led through the whole exercise to a rediscovery of one's own tradition in a deeper way. Even at a fairly prosaic level one can live tolerantly with the warts of one's own church when one has seen that other churches have theirs too!

I have often called myself an Anglican or a Protestant within the Catholic Communion and I continue to think of myself as such, but that, I am convinced, is the very best place for Anglicans and Protestants to be and the more of them there the better! I have no desire whatever to be an Anglican or a Protestant anywhere else. Indeed the prospect would be a very dreary one and I simply do not contemplate the possibility. And by the Catholic Communion I mean, of course, the Roman one too. I do not say this for the benefit of Anglicans or Protestants, who understand the position well enough, but for the type of fellow Catholic who is always trying to push people out of the church if they do not share his or her narrow ultramontanism. I was baptised into the full Catholic Communion by a bearded French missionary in Malaya within thirty-six hours of my birth and there I hope always to remain, enjoying the incredible riches of God's gifts in the fellowship not only of the Pope but of Archbishop Helder Camara and Mother Teresa and Barbara Ward and the Little Sisters of Jesus and the Benedictine nuns of Stanbrook. One could go on and on. Somewhat paradoxically, for on the one hand it is the sheer size and diversity of the Catholic communion which brings home to me its claim to be the best available embodiment of christian grace in the contemporary world, on the other my affections remain with the narrow little minority inheritance of our own English tradition. It has been a tradition of obstinate but not irrational non-conformity. Much as I admire the Church of England it has for me rather too much of the worldly self-confidence of an erastian establishment. The Catholic Church, of course, carries much the same ethos in some other countries and I am glad I do not belong to it there. Here in England we have been a little flock, foolish enough and intolerant too from time to time, yet still more persecuted than persecuting. The ecclesiastical tradition of Thomas More and Margaret Roper, Margaret Clitherow and Gertrude More, Mary Ward and Richard Challoner is not one I would exchange for any other. Let it never be forgotten that our succession was not an episcopal succession. It was one of laymen, indeed very often of laywomen. A. L. Rowse, who appears to dislike Catholics and women almost equally, believes that it was only the uppishness of Elizabethan women, improperly refusing to be dominated by their more erastian menfolk, which kept Catholicism alive at all.

It may well be so. And there's glory for you! I do not feel imperialist about this inheritance though perhaps I once did. I do not wish to thrust it down the throats of others. I find in ecumenical encounter so many other rich spiritual traditions to discover and admire and I have no doubt that they too have bred saints. But for me ecumenism has not led my heart away from the field in which God first set me.

There is a very real danger for those who take ecumenism as seriously as I have done of falling victim to a new form of over-churchly concern. I felt it sometimes at both Mindolo and Selly Oak and compared life in both those very pleasant places, a little unfairly, with an endless jolly interdenominational tea party on the vicarage lawn. The churches will be judged in very hard terms on their service to the world, their care for the needy, the poor, the oppressed. Nothing appalled me more than the easy ecumenism and pentecostal enthusiasms of white christians in South Africa which could leap every divide but that of colour. Yet I have to confess that I have never been much of a social worker; almost everything in my world is transformed into decidedly cerebral terms, but I have found myself forced more and more insistently by the inner logic of gospel and world to think out the former in terms of its task of liberation and to participate in that task in so far as I am capable. In the last few years I have done this principally through my links with the CIIR, the Catholic Institute for International Relations, and in relation to southern Africa. There are so many profoundly important causes in the world today that there has clearly to be very much of a division of labour among those who do genuinely care about any of them, so I find it strange and even self-condemning when people much involved in one cause blame people who have found their area of principal concern elsewhere. For me Africa and race relations have been my primary field ever since the early 1950s. It is, moreover, an area where people in Britain have a considerable collective responsibility deriving both from past history and from present investments, cultural links and personal relationships, so that we do have a very considerable capacity to influence things for change if we choose to do so. By and large we do not so choose. I found that the lay people working in the CIIR see things very much as I do and I have felt very much at home working with them on a variety of projects. I have found here a new cluster of close friends, and this has been all the more important as I have encountered no other Catholic institution in Britain (other than St Edmunds House) both willing to share its work with me and congenial in aim and inspiration.

I have indicated my attitude to these issues particularly in *Southern Africa and the Christian Conscience* and in *Wiriyamu*. It could be called a radical christian attitude, but it is fairly far from being a so-called 'marxist' one. The same is certainly true for CIIR. It may seem unnecessary to speak about this, yet a vigorous christian concern for social justice is so much misliked by those christians and non-christians who have been very satisfied to see the churches and their devout liturgies prop up any *status quo*, however oppressive, that they are willing to throw all the mud they can at any christian who does something to remove that prop. Fortunately in this matter one is today far from isolated: nothing is more encouraging than the deep change which is coming over the Catholic Church in this decisive field in many countries. There are so many lay people, nuns and priests so committed today to the struggle for justice, even at the cost of their lives, that one's own efforts seem extremely puny and uncostly in comparison.

Christian radicalism is in no way a marxist pheno-menon but derives from a straight recognition of the priorities of moral obligation as the gospel presents them to us. It can, of course, make greater or less use of marxist theory, and it can also be distorted by it. This is not surprising: every christian thinker makes use of some current philosophy and the subsequent synthesis is more or less valuable as an interpretation and personal appropriation of christian faith and of the riches of human understanding. There can be little doubt that marxism is today the philosophy that faces christians most significantly, though it is in reality not one but a maze of theories some of them now embedded as deeply in institutions of one sort and another as christianity itself. For some people marxism is the key for the liberation of mankind, and those people include many fervent christians; for others it is one of the most misguided and oppressive ideologies that man in his naïveté has ever succumbed to. All in all I belong to the second group of people rather than the first. I have no doubt that marxist social and economic analysis helps very considerably to understand the structures of oppression, but its failure to take sufficiently seriously the political, cultural and religious levels of human reality distorts its theoretical interpretations and has proved utterly disastrous in practice when marxists have come to power. Finally I see it as a vast over-simplification and I tremble for christians whom I love and admire when I see them carried away uncritically with enthusiasm for this latest instrument of spiritual and mental alienation.

I will illustrate how I see the approach of the christian radical with two examples – Portugal and Northern Ireland. In the problems of each the Catholic Church has been implicated and I have felt greatly concerned about both, although my personal involvement in Northern Ireland has been very slight.

It was almost by chance that I became so closely involved with the destiny of Mozambique. The CIIR's education committee, of which I am a member, was disturbed in 1973 to see the British government's plans to celebrate the sixth centenary of the so-called Anglo-

Portuguese alliance with a great show of friendship for the Portuguese government while the latter was involved in a long and brutal colonial war in Africa and entering into an ever closer military alliance with South Africa and Rhodesia. We resolved that in July at the moment of Marcello Caetano's visit to London we would hold a rather particularly responsible and weighty meeting, preferably in the House of Lords or at Chatham House, at which the speakers would assess all those sides of Portuguese policy about which our government was silent. We invited Mario Soares, then in exile in Paris, to be one of our speakers and Lord Caradon to be another, but we also needed someone more closely linked with the CIIR itself and able to talk particularly about Africa. For this task, after looking unsuccessfully elsewhere, we settled on myself. Consequently for some months before July I was preparing a suitable speech on Portuguese policy in Africa.

By chance, that May I visited Rhodesia to give lectures in various dioceses and while talking with the Spanish Burgos Fathers at work there I heard something of the problems of their brother missionaries in Mozambique, of the evidence they had of massacres by the army, and of the two priests of their society – Valverde and Hernandez – who were in a concentration camp near Lourenco Marques for protesting against these atrocities. Fortunately I was due to go to Spain the following month for an ecumenical conference at Salamanca, so I resolved to call in on the Generalate of the Burgos Fathers in Madrid to obtain more precise information. As a result of this I found myself at the beginning of July, just before Caetano's visit, in possession of a report in Spanish of the appalling massacre of Wiriyamu which had taken place only six months previously – 16 December 1972. The precision in this account of the wiping out of the population of a village a few miles from Tete was remarkable, over a hundred names of victims, mostly women and children, being listed. I had been assured by the Superior General of the Institute as to the reliability of the report and this seemed to me to be fully confirmed by the whole nature of the document. It had apparently never been published and the Portuguese authorities had rejected such protests on the subject as had privately been made. Nor was it an isolated case, for Valverde and Hernandez were in prison for their protests about a series of comparable, if smaller, massacres at Mucumbura in western Tete.

Once I was convinced of the accuracy of the report I realised both its considerable importance and my own grave responsibility in the matter. Its publication at that moment was likely to change the character of our Chatham House meeting a great deal, and CIIR was at first far from enthusiastic about it, but I felt that I had no option. I telephoned Louis Heren of *The Times* and sent him the document. He was at once convinced of its importance, like the able journalist he is, and agreed to publish it at once. It appeared on 10 July just a few days before Caetano's arrival. While awaiting its publication I had remarked to someone that I felt a little like Guy Fawkes standing by his powder barrels. My remark can hardly have been well understood for I had shown the document to no one except the translator from Spanish. Indeed I could hardly have appreciated its aptness myself, certainly I had not realised how great the explosion would be. At another time such a piece might pass with relatively little comment through the press, so hardened is the modern world to atrocities. In fact, as I found out later, it had been published in a small paper in Italy a month previously and had made no impact whatsoever. But on the front page of *The Times* less than a week before the arrival of the Portuguese Prime Minister in London it provoked an intense national and international storm. Even though I had in no way written the report and Mozambique was

8. With Mario Soares and Lord Caradon outside Chatham House, 11 July 1973.

one of the countries of Africa I had never worked in or visited at length, that storm centred about me. Strange as it seems looking back on it, the report had to stand or fall upon my credibility, my capacity to explain where it came from and to answer questions of any sort about it. I believe that it stood well enough. I saw my task not only as one of guaranteeing the report's full reliability but also of drawing out its inevitable implications for an assessment of Portuguese government, the wars of liberation in Portuguese Africa, and the role of the Church in countenancing (and occasionally criticising) colonial oppression. My defence of it took me, within ten days, to the United Nations – including a private interview with Secretary General Waldheim – and subsequently to several countries of western Europe.

Portuguese friends have assured me that the international storm over Wiriyamu had a good deal to do with the crumbling of Caetano's government and its overthrow by a military coup nine months later. The consequence was the rapid liquidation of Portuguese rule in Africa. Until then I had gone on trying to keep the matter before world opinion – indeed many of the eight different editions of my book, *Wiriyamu,* had still not appeared when the coup came in April 1974. From then on I began to appeal instead for some patience with Portugal's new leaders in the very difficult situation in which they found themselves while urging them, especially during the Spinola period, not to imagine that anything less than complete and speedy decolonisation could close a hopeless and horrid war.

I was perfectly well aware that this meant accepting marxist governments in Guiné Bissau, Mozambique and Angola for the simple and sufficient reason that their main nationalist movements were officially marxist. In the circumstances they could hardly be anything else, and those responsible for this state of affairs were certainly not the liberal supporters of these movements but the reactionary supporters of the fascist government in Lisbon which had blocked any other road to the independence of these countries. I had seen much of great value in Frelimo and I hoped – and still hope – that a fairly pragmatic and democratic type of African socialism would develop in these countries in due course. It may not, but there was anyway no alternative other than the temporary prolongation of an intensely cruel and unpopular racist regime. If the new regimes have their oppressive side, they may all the same be less tyrannical and a good deal more creative than many of the non-marxist governments, often backed by right wing christians in Europe, operating in other third world countries.

Essentially, as I have come more and more to see, the crucial issue in every country lies not between 'Right' and 'Left' but between the two poles of fascism and liberalism. Fascism can be of the right wing or of the left, and every regime – whatever its initial inspiration – is or becomes fascist when it destroys the basic structures of liberal government: an independent judiciary, legal means whereby the government may be peacefully changed by the governed, a free press, trade unions controlled by their members and not by the government or by party bosses. Underlying all this is the recognition of a plurality of moral authorities. Such things do not guarantee good government yet without them government is very unlikely to be good and it certainly will not cherish freedom. There is no quality of human life more important for the christian gospel than that of freedom and in the political order the institutions devised by the western liberal tradition seem to me by far the best means the human race has at its disposal for the safeguarding of liberty.

Some months after the Lisbon coup it started to look questionable whether there was going to be much of a future for freedom in Portugal or whether a left-wing military junta would not very quickly re-create a regime of oppression not unlike that which had been so joyfully overthrown. The Catholic Church in Portugal had for the most part been closely linked with the old regime and was finding it very difficult to adjust to the new conditions: it had a small, vociferous left wing but was otherwise rather uncreatively frightened of everything that was going on. Only the bishop of Oporto stood out as a rather old fashioned sort of liberal whom everyone had to respect but no one really agreed with. Yet in fact in the country there was a large majority of people that wanted the basic structures of a democracy more than anything else; it was fed up with unconvincing lectures from the heirs of Salazar and did not want to be back with the same sort of lectures given now by marxist army officers and members of the Communist party. These people were grouping in the Socialist and Social Democratic Parties, but at first they certainly lacked muscle.

The CIIR was as concerned as anyone about the situation and I twice visited Portugal in those months in order to understand better what was going on and see what we could do to help. The important thing was to give what support was possible to Portuguese democrats caught between the totalitarians of left and right and to encourage the Church to do so too. Of course many of the nicest and most sincere Catholics were ardent supporters of one or another of the extreme left-wing parties. These parties were, many of them, far more gentle in fact than the image they presented at that time, and I have no doubt that they played a very valuable part in the opposition to the old regime. I liked some of their members very much but I found their political judgment unreliable. Here as elsewhere, on observing the ease with which Catholics become marxists, I have wondered if it has something to do with the quasi-fascist and authoritarian background which many Catholics have grown up in.

The Communist grip on the Portuguese government grew steadily stronger during the first half of 1975 under the premiership of Vasco Goncalves, but so did popular opposition to it. My first visit to Lisbon had revealed to me that I now held a rather special position in Portugal: despite the control of the press under Caetano the significance of my Wiriyamu campaign had got through to the people of Portugal well enough. So when on 29 May in a letter to *The Times* I warned the military rulers of Portugal that despite their anti-fascist language they were heading rapidly back in a fascist direction, the BBC immediately transmitted my message on its Portuguese programme, and it was then reprinted in what remained of the free Lisbon press. Mario Soares and other friends told me that this letter had a quite considerable impact at a moment when the situation was still very flexible. Two months later, in July, I chanced to be able to stand on the platform with Soares at a vast demonstration in Lisbon in which, for the first time, he called for the resignation of Vasco. Some weeks later that resignation was secured — the opposition within the country, from Socialists and Catholics alike, had become overwhelming. Portugal is a poor country and it cannot recover quickly from the disharmonies created by decades of totalitarian rule and a colonial war which did as much harm to the mother country as it did to the colonies, but I am sure that in the premiership of Soares it set off on the right lines — peaceful, democratic, socialist, reconciling lines. Anything more socialistically revolutionary, while it might seem justified in view of the extreme poverty and economic underdevelopment of the Portuguese working class, would not only have been destructive of democratic structures but also profoundly alienating at the levels of culture and religion. Marxist revolution might not make Portugal economically richer, it would certainly make her culturally poorer. I have spoken at some length of Mozambique and

Portugal because for me personally my experience here was fairly decisive in working out an approach to contemporary politics and confirming earlier, less tested, hypotheses.

To turn to a problem far closer to home which deeply concerns us all. A christian in Britain today cannot possibly not feel involved in, and even in some way responsible for, the sectarian conflict of Northern Ireland, where Catholics continue to murder Protestants and Protestants murder Catholics, yet both churches dismiss the idea that they as christian bodies and the way they have consistently interpreted the gospel, hold prime responsibility for this appalling state of affairs. Here as elsewhere what is needed is an adequate analysis of the structure of a church in its impact upon society and in the particular way it has woven together a mass of religious and secular themes. Protestant (including Anglican) and Orange responsibilities are obvious enough, but I have no doubt that a very authoritarian Catholic Church has contributed almost equally to the trouble and is still doing far too little to resolve it. Leaving aside the ding-dong of historical controversy, a point which has seemed to me absolutely vital in the contemporary situation is the absence of all those human links proper to a shared community which derive from common schooling and mixed marriage. An essential part of the church model which Ultramontanism produced and tried to impose in mixed societies has been the segregation of Catholics from their non-Catholic brethren in as many areas of social life as is feasible. As deep a social ditch as possible is to be dug, but in no areas of life is it more important than those of education and marriage. Manning, the Ultramontane *par excellence,* struggled to keep Catholics out of Oxford and Cambridge and to found an absurd little university of his own in Kensington. At that level in Britain it did not work, nor at a good many other levels, so that in England

Catholics, while possessing adequate institutions to undergird their own sense of tradition and community, mix naturally enough at every level with their fellow nationals.

In Northern Ireland it worked a good deal more effectively (though still not at university level) under the pressures of an oppressive Protestant majority and the compact nature of the Catholic community. Protestant and Catholic bigotry, each of its own kind, have combined to create a society in which communal distrust is at a maximum and the bonds which normally draw groups together and work as a counter-balance to ideological separation, at a minimum. It is a strange thing that Protestant dominance and Irish nationalism, neither of them natural instigators of clericalism, have combined to provide clericalism in Ulster with more control over the Catholic community than it has almost anywhere else in the world. Ninety-eight per cent of Catholic children in Northern Ireland are in clerically controlled Catholic schools and there is only a handful of mixed marriages. Such a system has inbuilt long term consequences rather more frightening than its creators realised, a point I tried to make in a letter to *The Times* of 29 June 1977.

'People simply do not discriminate systematically against their school friends and brothers-in-law. It is the absence of almost all the normal social links which has made such profound group distrust possible and indeed inevitable. Inevitable because if two considerable communities inhabit the same towns, there are a limited number of possible patterns of relationship. A first is undisputed domination of one over the other, probably confining the latter to some sort of ghetto; a second is running conflict; a third is a reasonable measure of integration. If the bishops consistently oppose the third, they are opting for either the first or the second.

It is true that denominational schools do not always have these consequences. In many societies there are adequate alternative instruments of integration. Thus in England Catholic schools are not seriously divisive because the Catholic community is otherwise rather well integrated with its neighbours. But in a deeply divided context it becomes immeasurably important to use the relatively flexible instrument of schooling to reconcile and not to reinforce segregated loyalties. . . .

In many parts of the world the Catholic Church recognizes that there are compelling social reasons why Catholic children should not go to Catholic schools. What the bishops of Tanzania have accepted for one reason, why can the bishops of Ireland not accept for another?'

In supporting the *All Children Together* movement I quoted the Vatican Council, 'Parents who have the first and inalienable duty and right to educate their children, should enjoy true freedom in their choice of schools'.

In a similar way I have tried to show how it is of the very nature of marriage to be a socially reconciling relationship drawing people together across frontiers in a real covenant, and not only husband and wife but friends and relatives upon either side. Ban the inter-church marriage, as the Catholic bishops of Northern Ireland have in the past done their best to do, and you ban one of the main safety valves which make it possible for separate communities to live in a single province. One of the happiest weekends of my life was spent a year ago with ten or so couples of the Northern Ireland Mixed Marriage Association at Corrymeela on the Antrim coast. Take their heroic struggle upon the one hand to live together lovingly as Catholic and Protestant in circumstances where it is often hard even to find a house which they can inhabit with some security, and upon the other the bishop who refuses to give the sacrament of confirmation to Catholic children sent to non-Catholic schools by parents anxious to break down the psychological divide which is destroying their country. In one we find the reconciling and forgiving spirit of Christ manifestly present, in the other a line of action which can be described by no other adjective than 'wicked'. Yet has any other Catholic bishop in these islands had the courage to come out and say so and offer to confirm those children? I don't think so. Clerical solidarity takes primacy over the spirit of Christ.

I find it impossible to doubt that the parents in *All Children Together* are right and that they, not the bishops, are being guided here and now by the Spirit of God. This does not mean that all schools should necessarily be integrated there or elsewhere. The social divide would be effectively broken if even 30 per cent of the children upon either side had a genuinely mixed schooling. At the same time the positive values of the best Catholic schools would be retained. A nation is not well served by a monolithic educational pattern and where, as in England, denominational schools are not significantly divisive there is a very strong case for their retention in so far as they are good schools. The case has to rest upon excellence. My brother, Peter, is headmaster of a large Catholic secondary school in Leamington. His school is first class and widely recognised as such. I have no doubt that part of its excellence (but far from all of it) derives from the sense of identity and the educational philosophy which goes with its Catholic character. One would be a fool to want to do away with such a school. If the Catholic school can recognisably contribute to the community as well as to the Church, it is fully justified; where it is, all in all, socially harmful, there it should go. There is nothing in the nature of the Catholic Church which absolutely requires its ownership of schools or the presence of all Catholic children in such schools, and the claim that there is derives not from Catholicism but from clerical ultramontanism.

The most decisive and all pervading choice facing the Catholic Church today, both universally and in each diocese and parish, is that between freedom and illiberalism. Be it noted that reform is not incompatible with illiberalism by any means. Some 'progressive' parish priests appear almost more authoritarian in the imposition of their pet ideas on the laity than are many 'conservative' ones. Furthermore, while I have no doubt that Archbishop Lefebvre and his allies represent what was an extremely authoritarian wing of the Church in the day of its power, I yet greatly regret that they have been given much justification for their illiberal rejection of the second Vatican Council by the very illiberal and indeed shameful treatment of the Tridentine rite by Rome. I can see no conceivable justification for the banning of the full Tridentine rite and there seems something particularly unpleasing about its being banned by those ecclesiastics who, not so many years ago, showed themselves opposed to much milder measures of liturgical reform. The illiberalism of conformity and uniformity can as well take a 'progressive' as a 'conservative' face in the Church, just as it can in the state. In all its forms it needs to be confronted. If the Roman curia and so many bishops across the world were not so instinctively illiberal, we would most probably never have had the present threat of a double schism — Tridentinist on the one side, Ukrainian on the other.

It is naturally not a question of throwing over all sense of sound law but of getting priorities right. Traditionally, and still today, Catholics have had a preoccupation with 'authority' which is little less than neurotic. They find it astonishing to be told that freedom, not obedience, is the primary quality of the christian and should be a manifestly obvious characteristic of their Church. We still need a profound reorientation in spiritual values away from those proper to an ecclesiastical mirror of Hapsburg/Bourbon

Europe. Will the thousand flowers bloom as they could do in the post-Joannine church or will the system of a benevolent, watchful but at bottom ruthless ecclesiastical fascism be still maintained? Giving or withholding the cup from the laity, electing bishops or appointing them all from Rome, allowing Catholic children to go to non-catholic schools in strife-torn Belfast or refusing confirmation to those who do, accepting the call of a married man to the priesthood and the desire of a priest to enter in love into the sacrament of marriage or thrusting such people far from the ministry, all these and many other issues are essentially expressions of the conflict between a responsible christian freedom and clerical illiberalism. If the Church is to be an effective servant of freedom and justice in the wider society, as it is trying quite hard to be these days, it cannot continue internally to be a reserve of spiritual illiberalism.

In life there always comes a time when an issue, first perceived upon the horizon and then at steadily closer range, finally reaches a proximity of such personal significance that it can no longer be left as a matter merely to think or talk about. One cannot liberate without being liberated, teach without being taught, call to arms without oneself responding to the call. The issue of freedom and law, central to the New Testament, has reached me now not as a matter of exegesis but as a matter of existence. It is of the nature of law to be concerned with particulars and the particulars which have finally seemed insufferable to me in the light of the gospel, which is the master of all law, are simple enough. Liturgically there came a moment when I could not go on saying out loud the words of Christ 'Drink of this, all of you' and then gulping down the Cup of Christ's blood all alone because church authority told me to. Faced with every reason to marry and many years of desire to do so, the Church's denial to me and to a million others of this basic human right has become a symbol of the dominance of illiberalism not only in my own life but in that of Christ's church. The church of freedom has become in too many things the church of law. There comes a moment when the spirit of freedom within one cries 'Abba, Father' and one is prepared to tolerate it no more.

I have still to say something about the development of my attitudes to celibacy particularly in the 1970s. In the preceding decade when I argued in Africa in season and out of season for the creation of a diversified ministry with a large core to it of married priests, I tended to say that we should not be preoccupied with the personal problems of European and North American priests, even that these were clouding the true issue which was a systemic and structural one. There was something in that; nevertheless it was a one-sided viewpoint and from about 1969 I realised that I had got to face up to the other side of the issue – the increasing wave of withdrawals from the priesthood with the sort of profound personal problems which this revealed, problems apparently more or less inherent in the attempt to combine compulsory celibacy with the work and life style expected of an active priest today often living on his own.

One other white priest had joined Masaka diocese after me, a young Belgian. He had been an excellent priest, immensely hard working and zealous, a fluent preacher in Luganda. I expect he grew very lonely. It was when he left the priesthood to marry a Ugandan girl in 1969 that something broke through to me and I realised that I had to face up personally to what was going on. I had by then been a priest for 14 years. It was not just an issue of ministerial problems, educational levels, financial resources, but one of individual human beings. My closest friend at school became a priest in Westminster archdiocese, a gentle and much loved curate in central London. He has gone. Several of the friends I had at Oxford who entered the priesthood with such enthusiasm have gone. Of the fourteen young men who began 'Philosophy' at Broome Hall in 1949, only five were ordained as White Fathers; three of those five have gone. Of the four young priests living with me at the Beda in 1956 two have gone. I could continue with those ordained at Propaganda, white and black priests working with me in Africa, friends I have made since returning to England. In every single group the fall out has been very considerable and has included some of the ablest and most zealous. While many of these men would now certainly not wish to return to the priesthood under any circumstances, it is certain that a fair number of those who have married are anxious to do so. In England, for instance, they have constituted their own little fellowship, the *Advent Group*. I do not believe that the Church would be corrupted by welcoming back such men into its ministry, but I think that it is corrupted now by the torture this issue is producing in the lives of so many of its priests, those who finally stay as much as those who go, and by the *insouciance* ecclesiastical authority demonstrates in regard both to the pain and to the subsequent work of men trained for years and years in its seminaries.

Returning to Britain in 1970, drifting increasingly loose of any clerical structure though still passionately committed to the sense of the priesthood, I had to ask where I myself stood in all this. A personal reassessment is, I think, natural in one's early forties. I noticed how many of my friends left the priesthood about the age of 43 and then I remarked that it was just the same age that Newman and Manning had become Catholics, so I came to suspect that men, or perhaps just religious men, are inclined to hit a life crisis at that point and this observation certainly helped me through those particular years! The crisis, so far as I was concerned, was one in part of clerical life style, in part of sex and marriage, in part of the deepest matters of christian belief. As regards the first, this book as a whole illustrates how I have steadily lost confidence in the value of the clerical way of life such as I had largely accepted it at the time of ordination. I expect that this is true of many priests, who manage nevertheless to keep going fairly satisfactorily so long as they have a worthwhile particular job to do.

This does not mean that I have lost confidence in the human tradition of the Catholic priesthood. On the contrary. I have known many priests whom I have greatly admired some of them very wise and holy people. I remain grateful to have been allowed to share their company, even if I now question many of the clerical norms they mostly took for granted. But I want the tradition to be reformed so that it can be continued, rather than to see it go on crumbling unhappily away. Under the strains of the post-conciliar church my own old seminary of Propaganda Fide has effectively been closed and a tradition of over 300 years terminated. That does not please me and I don't believe it was a happy or a necessary decision. It was rather an expression of the inability of curialists to bend with sensitivity and understanding to new winds. Unable to bend, they had to break. Equally in England the tradition of the Catholic clergy will only be saved if rescued from the narrow stipulations of ultramontanes. The more the model of Manning is held up as the model of catholicity, the more the priesthood is bound by a tight clericalism, the less hope there can be. Of course I am arguing now for a great deal more than a retreat from the consequences of 19th century ultramontanism: this was, after all, but one more wave in a far older Roman tide. But it is really the final model which makes plain a much lengthier development. It is, in some ways, to the days before the Gregorian reform of the 11th century that I would now have us find the courage to return, and that is, admittedly, a long way.

My own, somewhat accidental, evolution away from

any effective attachment to a particular diocese has doubtless brought me to a more declericalised type of priesthood than I would seriously propose to others, though I do think the Church is a good deal richer for a few wandering lollards. Anyway from this point of view I have come through my 'life crisis' by partially opting out of the clergy, but not from my commitment to the priesthood, and I find little theoretical difficulty in this, though admittedly in practice it is not easy to exercise the priesthood in the Catholic Church of Britain today in a genuinely non-clerical way; as a consequence, there is some danger, it could seem, of my priesthood slowly atrophying, though I doubt whether that will happen.

The level of sex and marriage proves a more difficult one to cope with. To begin with it was, as they say, 'sublimated'. In fact that is not too accurate. On one side it remained consciously present, a sort of immature temptation, something fairly easily held in order. On another, my normal heterosexual tendencies blocked over the years of any natural outlet subtly transposed themselves for a large part into horrible and quite unnatural fantasies of a sadistic and masochistic kind. I was wholly unprepared for this – no one in the seminary thought to prepare one for what can happen to 'sublimated' sexuality, and for long I understood it very little myself. The almost completely male society in which I lived and in which any sort of sexual release was effectively clamped down produced instead a mental state which at one time seemed not far short of madness. Fortunately when I ceased to work in a seminary these things slowly passed and I can even be grateful for them now in that they widened my area of human sympathy and psychological understanding. And that is why I mention them. I suspect that this sort of thing happens to a fair number of priests and that most would hardly dare admit it or turn for help. When I did try once in fairly early days to explain what was going on to a priest who seemed to me unusually wise and experienced and was giving a clergy retreat, I found no understanding at all, and I did not try again.

So it was only in my late thirties when I was moving back into a more sexually mixed world, especially after being posted to Mindolo in 1968, that my inner sexuality gently readjusted too and I began to realise how much I wanted to marry. At Oxford and for many years afterwards all my friendships had been with men. Now on the contrary I found it impossible to be very interested in any male friendship while my need for female relationships seemed to encompass every side of my life and thinking with a profound craving, most of which was not physical. While women friends came to help me more and more in these years, such relationships could only partially cope with the frustration and a deep depression and sadness that had settled over me. My sisters and sisters-in-law had long played a very important role in my life; they were joined now from time to time by other women with some of whom I fell less or more in love. It is clear from my own experience that if some priests may have fallen victim to women on the search for an ordained husband, many others will have been helped and even upheld in their priesthood by the patience and understanding of women they have come close to.

I could hardly not think a good deal about marriage at this time. I was after all for two and a half years engaged upon a full-time study of it in its African context. I was also in close contact with the Inter-Church Marriage Association. Through both these experiences coupled with my personal struggles I matured to become, I hope, a very much more balanced person: someone who had at last been seriously affected by the needs and insights of the female half of the world – which was certainly not the case until I had passed my mid-thirties. The almost desperate yearning for sex and marriage of some years ago seems now to have

passed. It was held in check at the time simply by my conviction that as a priest it must not be and therefore could not
be. Today I yearn much less but am, perhaps, a good deal
better prepared for the most difficult but wonderful of
voluntary relationships. I no longer crave female friendship
in a sort of starved manner and find that close new friends
are at least as likely to be men as women. But I do
immeasurably value female insight and love as one of the
most splendid things which a man can find upon earth,
especially when offered and accepted in the covenant of
marriage. Things have fallen into position in my mind and
heart as for years they did not. Of course it remains a strain,
a very considerable one, formally to reject a basic pre-
supposition that has hitherto controlled one's life. Yet to do
so when one is convinced that it is right can be very liberating too. I cannot see a much nobler challenge than to show
that the call of christian marriage is not a call away from
that of the priesthood and the service of God, but that there
is a profound harmony between the two which can fittingly
be lived within the framework of a single life and inside the
Catholic Communion.

I hope and pray the Church or its bishops will not try to
excommunicate me for responding to that call but, to be
frank, nothing they can do will deter me, though it can
greatly hurt me. When one has seen before one the clash
of law and gospel freedom, one cannot abandon freedom
for law whatever the penalties. The words of Grosseteste,
greatest of English medieval bishops and himself a high
papalist, ring in my ears. When faced with what he considered the wholly immoral demand that he provide the
Pope's nephew with a benefice in his diocese, he found that
in conscience he could stand no more:

> 'Out of the obedience and fealty by which I am
> bound, as a child to his parents, to the most Holy
> Apostolic See and the love I bear to its union with the
> Body of Christ, filially and obediently I do not obey, I

    reject, I rebel. . . .'

To arrive at this conclusion, this ability personally to appropriate Grosseteste's seemingly so paradoxical position, has meant years and years of struggle with conscience, intellect and affections about the meaning of priesthood, marriage, sexuality, freedom, the immediate and most urgent pastoral needs of the third world church. I am immensely glad that I have come to this conclusion but I am glad too that in the long journey to it I have been permitted to cut no corners.

There is a far deeper level at which too one has had to struggle with the meaning of life, that of one's basic christian faith and understanding. When I was in the seminary I seem to have had few problems about the absolute reliability of central Catholic doctrine. I have always seemed more intellectually concerned with the social and the institutional than with the spiritual and the philosophical. In fact this is only partly true for the heart of my concern has been with how the spiritual can be embodied in the social. Certainly my interest in the institution as such has long been waning while behind social preoccupations, however pressing, has been an at times agonizing struggle with spiritual ultimates – the reality of God, the authority of Christ, the meaning of the Resurrection, survival of death. On each of these there has been a battle and it is not over. All I can say is that one is carried on. Perhaps I understand a good deal less than formerly, but I trust rather more. If at times it has seemed very hard to go on believing in anything, disbelief would signify for me disintegration and an appalling hopelessness. And it would be wholly unjustified. God, Christ, the Eucharist have been the decisive realities of my life. Without them nothing would make any sense to me at all. I can only pray that this great gift of faith, wholly unmerited, God will never take from me.

How God handles each of us is far beyond our

understanding. I find that I have been blessed with things of the spirit just as I have been blessed with things of earth – home, health, education, family love – in a way seemingly much above what is fair or balanced. But what is fair? For long I agonized over the innocent peasants massacred at Wiriyamu with whose fate in a strange way my life was for a while entwined. To uphold their cause even in death and, through them, that of all the other victims of this world's misery was the plainest of duties. And yet the gap remains. The lines of the American, Stephen Vincent Benet, come back at me unanswerable:

> Out of the moiling street,
> With its swelter and its sin,
> Who has given me this sweet?
> And given my brother dust to eat?
> When does his wage come in?

All one can do is give back, as generously as one may, all one has been given. I have certainly not done this very well, and yet in retrospect one finds the more one tries to give, the more still one receives. The last personal justification for celibacy I located here: in so many things I am and have always been a 'have', taking for granted as almost my own the loveliest things of this world. It was good, I felt, to be a 'have not' at least on one hard central point: to have no wife. I can only ask forgiveness if, finally, I should deny the negation of the cross where most insistently it pressed upon me. Yet I do not really believe in adopting patterns of asceticism, of negation, for the sake of negation. When there is sound reason to take on something and that thing is hard, one rightly finds in it the shadow of the Cross and believes that the very pain can be fruitful. Or when suffering comes involuntarily to one, as to us all it does. It is a different thing to hold it to be according to the mind of Christ to seek the cross simply for the sake of the cross. When celibacy seemed, all in all, justified or at least a necessary burden for the sake of the community, one could rightly accept it as a voluntary sharing in Christ's suffering. When one's rational judgment has gone at last decisively the other way, it would be perverse, I believe, even a twisted form of spirituality, to hold on to it simply as an instrument of personal mortification.

So instead I have resolved to step out, as boldly as I may, on a new course but not a new faith. I could hardly have the courage to do this if I did not have the hope that in due course I will share this life with another. Yet it remains very much a decision taken on its own and alone. One should not even partially push onto someone else the onus of facing up to one's own past commitments. It has in all honesty taken me long enough to face up to them and to decide that in the Church as elsewhere there is a time for personal risk, for applying to oneself the old lines of Montrose:

> He either fears his fate too much,
> Or his deserts are small,
> That dares not put it to the touch,
> To gain or lose it all.

Yet the winning and the losing are not in man's hands. There is no text of the gospel so painfully close to my heart as those words in Matthew 'What does it profit a man if he gain the whole world and suffer the loss of his own soul?' What does it indeed? Both gain and loss are finally in God's hands alone, and it is fortunate for us all, theologians and agnostics, popes and heresiarchs, martyrs and lollards, that it is so. To him who is all comprehending and all forgiving one can but confide one's cause, knowing that in so far as it is acceptable it must cease to be one's own, indeed that it never was so: his truth, his freedom, his reconciling love – understood or misunderstood, these are the only things that at bottom can rightly move one, but once moved, once put one's hand to the plough, one may not then turn back.

3

Can the Pope be Wrong?
Humanae Vitae and the Church (1968)

The most striking effect of the encyclical *Humanae Vitae* may be seen as one of turning a controversy about moral theology into a controversy about ecclesiology – that is to say, about what the Church is. The moral theology debate will, of course, continue but this forthright reiteration by a papal encyclical of a theological view rejected by a large proportion of Catholic theologians and millions of lay people all over the world has brought clearly into question the whole nature of the Church's teaching authority: the function of the Holy See, the function too of the world's episcopate, and – perhaps even more clearly – of the *consensus fidelium*: the common mind of the faithful, the collective judgement of the people of God.

This is happening, of course, not just because of what Catholics – far more Catholics than the Pope realized – had already come to hold, but because of the theological inadequacy of the encyclical itself. Its argumentation has only too clearly failed to commend its conclusion. Yet its very weight as an important papal document presented for the instruction of the entire Church, and even the entire world, on a matter of urgency, truly involving the lives and happiness of so many millions of people, prevents one anymore from keeping silence. It has forced one, as nothing else could, to state in all sincerity where one stands, to witness publicly and as a matter of conscience (as one had trusted never to have to do) that in one's personal judgement a teaching of the living Pope is not God's will for the living Church, that – at the very least – the use of contraception within marriage is not always objectively immoral.

Undoubtedly this is the position of many dedicated Catholic priests and laity today, but the definite and public rejection of a central teaching in a papal document of this kind by men standing within the Roman communion (and determined to remain there) involves one most necessarily in a new look at what the Church is. Can a Roman Catholic take such a step? Does not Roman Catholic ecclesiology involve one necessarily in accepting such a solemn piece of teaching, or – if one cannot accept it – in leaving the Catholic communion?

To answer such vital questions, we must study the nature of the witness to God's truth which the Church is able and called upon to provide, and this within the context of her entire life. We can do this best by comparing the teachings of Vatican II with the practice of the Church, both pre- and post-conciliar.

The heart of the Council's ecclesiological teaching can be summed up in two words: Communion and Collegiality. The visible Church is a eucharistic fellowship – a society of men made continually one by sharing in the sacrament of Christ's sacrificial death and resurrection. The meal they participate in can only be such a sacrament – the true renewal of the eternal covenant – to those who believe. It is essentially a fellowship of believers; it is entered into by the visible rite of baptism; its constant cause in the visible order, focal point, and symbol of essential meaning, is the sacrament of the Eucharist. The Church is God's explicit people; and men can claim that they are such because of the covenant relationship God has established with them in Christ, and we find that one, eternal Covenant present and renewed in every Eucharist.

The Eucharist is a necessarily local event, and celebrating in it the mystery of Christ is a local fellowship: a local church. The Church, we can say, is always local and never local. It is essentially local because the local eucharistic fellowship really has all the basic characteristics of the Church, and yet it is never local because the covenant is one for all. It is the covenant of the universal Saviour, the Church is his one body, and men entering it anywhere enter it everywhere. The Church is not simply the local communion, she is the world communion. Yet the character of the world communion is determined by its being a fellowship of local communions. The churches form the Church, and only by being themselves – the Church here and now, a fellowship of these men in this particular society – can the Church be herself, truly Catholic, truly taking on the qualities of all men, in some sort of image and continuation of the Incarnation.

The Catholic Church is a full communion of local churches, a communion of the sacraments and of faith. Among the sacraments is that of orders, the sacrament of a particular ministry instituted by Christ in the Twelve. This commissioned ministry of the Apostles, their ordained assistants and successors, is part of the structure of the Church. Its essential role is to preside at the Eucharist, to preach with authority, to present the very model of service within the Servant Church (*Constitution on the Church*, Art. 18). But it is not the only ministry and it strengthens but cannot replace the total mission of the people of God. By baptism and confirmation all Christians are consecrated to share actively in the one royal priesthood of the new covenant, the priesthood of Christ. The prophetic, priestly and royal functions of the Church have to be exercised (and are only adequately exercisable) through the various activities of worship and mission of the whole people (*Constitution on the Church*, Arts. 10-12, 34-36). The total mission of the Church is exercised and manifested through a whole variety of ministries: not only apostles, but prophets, teachers, healers, helpers, administrators (I Corinthians 12:28; Ephesians 4:11; see *Constitution on the Church*, Art. 18, *Decree on the Lay Apostolate*, Arts. 2 and 3). Nor are the non-hierarchical ministries to be looked upon as entirely secondary, a sort of 'compensation prize.' The Church of God, Saint Paul remarks, is built upon both apostles and prophets, but the cornerstone is Christ (Eph. 2:20).

The function of the hierarchy is not to dominate and monopolize the ministry, but to provide a God-given backbone to the life of the Church in sacramental life, in pastoral service and in teaching. The local church is not synonymous with its minister though it can be most easily seen and identified in the person of its minister and it cannot function as a full church without the apostolic ministry. As there is one Church, so there is one hierarchical ministry. It is not an aggregation of local ministries, conceived somehow federally, but an organic unity such that the apostolic ministry in particular places is a sharing in the one corporate ministry given by Christ to the Twelve. The One Church has one ministry and apostolic authority, and the bishops of particular dioceses both represent Catholic unity and apostolicity at the local level and represent their own diocese, their particular church, to the whole people of God.

The collegiality of bishops is the reverse side of the communion of churches and one cannot exist without the other. The collegiality of bishops is itself but one, uniquely important, expression of the collegiality of Christian life at every level – the *presbyterium,* the total ministerial body of the diocese, led by its bishop; the parish led by its parish priest; the religious order led by its elected head. Collegiality is not, at its root, a matter of law, though it needs legal expression (and can at times be ignored, denied, or inadequately realized by legal formulas). It is a matter of Christian living, the expression at the level of action, ministry, community thought, of the fellowship, the *Communion.*

The Communion is necessarily, and highly desirably, a union of diversity. This is true even of the local eucharistic assembly. It unites, but it unites those who are and remain diverse – in character, occupation, culture. At the same time the local church, being the fellowship of these people here in this age and land, takes on itself a particular character. It produces its own prayer and liturgical forms; its own characteristic expressions of Christian thought and theology; it develops its own structural pattern, trains its priests according to the particular needs of Christian life and witness in its own circumstances.

The Church cannot grow healthily nor function properly in her several parts, nor balance respect for the local community with loyalty to the *Una Catholica,* without living this truth of the communion of churches. Yet it is a single and a full communion. The unity of communion, of the one whole, is as overwhelmingly important as the diversity within the communion. Despite the diversity, the Church of God is essentially a single communion, a single visible fellowship with unity of faith and love, of worship and witness. The unity is guaranteed especially by the hierarchical communion of the ordained ministry. This is the unity of the episcopal college in and with its head, the bishop of Rome. The college of bishops has replaced the college of apostles; the pope, a bishop among bishops, has replaced Peter, an apostle among apostles, in that unique function entrusted to Peter of being within the group the divinely appointed focus and full bearer in himself of the total ministry entrusted to all. There is not a double ministry here, a double authority. One authority is to be found in the whole episcopal college united with the bishop of Rome, and in the bishop of Rome, head of that college.

This collegial structure of hierarchical authority mirrors the being of the whole Church, a communion of churches which it was created to serve; it can only function fruitfully and to the mind of Christ while it is effectively faithful to itself. That is to say, in so far as hierarchical authority fails to act according to its character of ministry and seeks instead to dominate, or fails to act according to its collegial character, and behaves monarchically, or again fails to act according to its disinterested character and becomes a tool of worldly self-seeking – in so far as these things happen, the hierarchical ministry of the Church is failing to do what Christ intended of it. Being a human Church such failings have happened, do happen, and will continue to happen without however even at the worst moments ever totally corrupting the ministry, any more than they can totally corrupt the Church. She is and she always will be a Church of sinners and of fools, and yet the body of Christ, the temple of the Holy Spirit.

Corruptions are easier to spot when they represent an obvious moral failing of a personal kind, but they may be at least as opposed to the kingdom of heaven when, despite a genuine religious character, they represent in truth a failure to understand the Church's real mission or the Christ-given character and limitations of hierarchical ministry. Failings of understanding involving the nature of the Church's mission, usurpations by Church authority of functions or realms of competence not confided to it by Christ or, again, involving a false conception of the way in which right ends can be achieved within the Church; such failings have resulted in the past in as unchristian things as the continual harassing of Jews in the Papal States, all the scandal of the Roman Inquisition, in occasion after occasion when at local or world level the power of the Church has been used in history to do the devil's work. This does not mean, of course, that there have not been many other occasions when the power of the Church and of the papacy has been used to do God's work – to speak the truth without fear or favour, to challenge tyranny, feed the hungry, protect the Jews. The Catholic does not need to be convinced of that or to explain it. What he does have to face up to are the too many times when the contrary has been the case.

It is the whole Church which is the pillar and witness to revealed truth. There is no inherent reason to think that the faith lies purer in the soul of a bishop or a theologian than of a committed lay christian. All have received the gift of the Spirit of truth, all bear witness to that truth once delivered to the saints; at the intellectual level the communion of the baptized is signified by a *consenus* in the faith. It is not easy to judge of this *consensus*. When the passing of time and development in society and thought present to men new problems, new questions as to what is and what is not acceptable to the mind of Christ, there is no easy way through for the Church of God. There is no oracle to which men can turn; only by honest living and prayer and discussion and an openness to the Holy Spirit can the Church (hierarchy and laity combined) come little by little to an understanding of what is and what is not implied in the once delivered message of salvation. We are the people of God, a human people, and all our processes – both of mission and communion – have to be done through the normal movements of human living and thinking. The inspiration of the Holy Spirit works through such processes. It does not bypass them. Among men there is no short cut to certainty nor is there in the Church. The normal ultimate way whereby the mind of Christ will be definitely expressed will be by a decision of an ecumenical council or by the Pope, head of the episcopal college, exercising the fullness of his teaching authority. But this has to come as the expression of a genuine ecclesial *consensus*. The mind of the Church becomes clear through the process whereby the *sensus fidelium* (the mind of the faithful) within the many local churches grows little by little into a *consensus ecclesiarum* (the common witness of the churches). This, formulated and expressed by the chief pastors of those churches, becomes a *consensus episcoporum,* the witness of the bishops of the one Catholic Church in and with their head, the bishop of Rome.

Attempts to short-cut this process, to ignore the reality of the Church as a communion of churches, to treat it as if it were but a single Church ('The Church of Rome' as non-Catholics mistakenly call us), to regard the Pope as an oracle who can, apart from human processes and the in-built constitution of the Church, pontificate with certainty upon any subject, is to misunderstand what the Church of God is, to make of the Pope what he is not, and to lead the faithful grievously astray. The condemnation of Pope Honorius by an ecumenical council and its ratification by Pope Agatho is surely in itself sufficient evidence of the fact that the Pope can err. And we have in fact a whole tradition of erring papal teaching: Gregory II's several points in a solemn letter of 726 to Saint Boniface on moral questions in the Church of Germany; Pope Innocent IV's justification of torture; Pope Urban's treatment of Galileo; Gregory XVI's condemnation of freedom of conscience in the encyclical *Mirari Vos* of 1832; frequent teachings of the Pontifical Biblical Commission in our own century; and much else.

In practice we often cannot have an ecumenical council or an infallible papal utterance, and we have to live in this world of sense and this life of faith with the possibility of religious error. The real danger is not that possibility but the creation of a system which is mistakenly thought to eliminate it, the treating of fallible teaching as if it were infallible, and the restriction of the teaching authority to a single central ministry, acting almost in isolation and in a semi-oracular way.

The mistake in regard to the *magisterium,* the teaching ministry in the Church, has been akin to that concerning ministry generally: the creation of an ever more rigid pattern, making a central part of the ministry do the work of the whole. Just as historically the presbyterate has tended to eat up every other ministry, making all 'lay' members of the Church into passive 'receiving' members, 'sheep', instead of its acting as a stimulus and focal point for the many ministries of the local church; so in the course of history, the tendency was to reduce the *magisterium* more and more to its central core: the Petrine See. The *sensus fidelium* was reduced almost to meaninglessness, while the bishops became in practice little more than papal mouthpieces, the spokesmen for encyclicals. So far as possible they were trained in Rome, the better to have a completely Roman point of view. The reduction of the Catholic Church in practice to the Roman Church – never, of course, effectively achieved, but the tendency was quite clear – was a denial of the real constitution of the People of God.

From that denial, from the governmental, monarchical, monolithic conception of the Church that was dominant above all in the fifty years following Vatican I, Vatican II has delivered us – giving expression instead to the traditional, balanced, Catholic conception of the Church in which communion and ministry, local church and world church, laity and episcopate and Petrine See all have their proper place.

It is one thing to proclaim a teaching (particularly when

it is done in a long-winded way without pressing the implications that many people brought up in a different world would have found unpalatable); it is another to translate it into a way of life and the institutional processes of a vast community. It is perfectly obvious that the way the Church has been governed in the eighty years preceding Vatican II has not been in accordance with the implications of Vatican II's teaching. It was governed on the assumption that supreme authority lay with the Pope alone, that he was competent to judge upon any matter concerning the whole Church or any local church with a minimum of consultation; that the laity had no function to speak but only to listen and that once the Pope had spoken on any matter – be it Anglican orders or the existence of Limbo – it would then be highly impious for any Catholic further to question such teaching, at least publicly.

Such an ecclesiology was not a Catholic one and it is not compatible with the full teaching of Vatican II. But what has to be noted here is that Vatican II having passed, the Pope and many of the bishops do not seem to be aware that the central teaching of this ecumenical council requires from them a seriously different way of acting and of conceiving the papal function from what was accepted before.

It is perfectly true that in apparent concern with the implementation of the collegial principle, the Pope laid down some rather restrictive norms for the meeting from time to time of a synod of bishops. But when the synod first met in 1967, it became clear that it was not really desired to make of it a body to discuss and decide the most important matters facing the Church today. In the post-conciliar era these were undoubtedly two: clerical celibacy and birth control. Instead of discussing these two decisively important matters, both of which vitally concern the lives of millions of Christians the world over, the synod was limited either to a very general discussion of the total content of faith, or to acting as a sort of rubber stamp to approve relatively minor and basically uncontroversial directives implementing the Council's decisions on liturgy, seminary training and so on.

At the same time the publication of the encyclicals *Mysterium Fidei, Sacerdotalis Caelibatus,* and *Humanae Vitae* shows with absolute clarity that Rome intends to continue the basic ruling and teaching of the Church in a quite un-collegial manner. That is to say, in practice, though Rome accepted from the Council certain specific points of reform it is continuing to try to run the Church in a basically pre-conciliar manner. It is treating the Church, not as a communion of churches with the Pope as 'the supreme judge of inter-church relations' (*Decree on Eastern Catholic Churches,* Art. 4) but as if it were one only Church of Rome, unified not by a full communion but by simple obedience to a single government. And many bishops are only too happy to acquiesce in this return to the post-Vatican I pattern.

If one believes that the great themes of Vatican II were truly signs given under the inspiration of the Holy Spirit for the renewal of Christian living in our time, not only by adaptation to the circumstances of today, but also by a greater fidelity to the whole revelation and the totality of Catholic Christian tradition than was apparent in preceding years, then a deliberate refusal to implement these themes in practice is surely the most likely condition possible to produce a lack of receptivity to the guidance of the Holy Spirit here and now.

And this is surely just what happened. In the encyclical *Humanae Vitae,* Pope Paul did something which in the history of Christian doctrine is almost without parallel. He attempted to lay down unchanging principles of morality without any reference to revelation. Admitting the absence of support in the latter he endeavoured to base himself upon natural law and human reason. But such a foundation precisely requires to be recognised as such by men of good will. Yet this is just what is lacking. His own theologians (the minority within the Papal Commission) had to admit that the natural law foundation for forbidding contraception cannot be established by reason but only by authority. Yet the living authority of the Church has no power to draw up doctrines of its own. It can only interpret what comes from God, and it can only know what comes from God by revelation backed by demonstrable reason. The teaching authority of the Church is correlative with revelation (*Constitution on the Church,* Art. 25; *Constitution on Divine Revelation,* Art. 10). The Council spoke of it entirely within the context of "preaching the gospel" and "bringing forth from the treasure of revelation things new and old." The content of the Church's authentic teaching today cannot be justified in terms of what the Church taught yesterday unless this can itself be shown as truly constituting a bringing forth of the treasure of revelation.

In the present case neither revelation nor convincing reason is forthcoming. The Pope put himself in the position of taking sides against the convinced conscience of millions of lay Catholics, against the theological conviction of many leading theologians, against the strong advice of numerous bishops. By refusing to allow the problem to be discussed by the Ecumenical Council or by the synod of bishops, by rejecting the advice of a large majority of his own commission together with a Resolution of the World Congress of Catholic Laity, he placed himself in the position of an oracle.

This was bad ecclesiology. It cannot be regarded as surprising if, when a Pope, with however sincere intentions, so totally ignores the ecclesial 'signs of the times' placed before him, and acts in a manner which accords neither with the conduct of a normal prudent man nor with the known constitution of the Church as an ecumenical council has just delineated it, God permits him to make a bad mistake, just as he has – without any possibility of doubt – permitted many Popes to make such mistakes in the past. The Pope's function is to be a focus for the total life of the Church, not a substitute.

If such a thing can happen, it does not involve a breakdown in Catholic ecclesiology. On the contrary, it is part of it. The Pope is Simon Peter and his function in the Church cannot be taken away. 'Thou art Peter and upon this rock I will build my Church' (Matt. 16:18). Every text in Scripture has its significance, and this text and similar passages pointing to Peter's unique ministry are not to be explained away. But nor are other texts which also throw light upon the mystery of the Petrine function in the Church. He said to Peter, 'Get behind me, Satan! You are a hindrance to me; for you are not on the side of God, but of men' (Matt. 16:23). This terrifyingly strong passage is as relevant as Matthew 16:18, in explaining the position of Peter and his successors in the historic Church. Neither records merely a fact of history; both throw light upon the total character of the papal phenomenon. If one cannot consider it unimportant and insignificant for subsequent Christians that the gospel calls Peter the rock and again the support of his brethren, one cannot consider it of no significance that Christ also once called him Satan. And the saying has been passed down to every one of us. The greater the role given to a man, the more serious the consequences of its misuse. That this has happened in history one cannot doubt. The gospel seems to warn us that the function of the rock does not exclude its bearer – even a most holy bearer – from at times leading gravely astray. An ecclesiology which leaves no room for this possibility would seem to be less than faithful to the totality of Scripture.

We are shown the same thing yet again in the Epistle to the Galatians, when Peter was already Pope: 'When

Cephas came to Antioch I opposed him to his face, because he stood condemned' (Gal. 2:11). He stood condemned by Paul when he stood with the conservatives, the party of circumcision. Every historical situation has its own existential differences, but if we are to believe that passages in Scripture have relevance for Christian life in after ages, then these passages can warn us not to create for ourselves an ecclesiology in which the successor of Peter would be in all concrete circumstances infallible and unrebukable. On the contrary, they are telling us that there will be times when Peter has to be rebuked – not for the immorality of his personal life, but because his thoughts and way of behaviour, though sounding religious enough, are not of God.

To believe this is fully compatible with every doctrine of the Catholic Church, indeed it is required thereby. Certainly there is no simple formula for Christian living, 'for now we see in a mirror dimly' (1 Cor. 13:12). Collegiality alone does not solve all our problems and Councils too have committed serious errors. Episcopal collegiality itself would be misunderstood if not seen within the context of the true dependence of the *magisterium* upon revelation, of the positive significance of the *sensus fidelium,* and of the necessarily partial character of human thoughts and utterances.

But if we understand these things aright, and try to live them within the one full Catholic communion of the great Church, then at least in faith and prayer we may hope that the Holy Spirit will not leave us upholding as orthodoxy what is clearly untenable. But if we do not, if we insist on acting according to an ecclesiology which is clearly not that of an ecumenical council which has taught us for four long years, then indeed we cannot be surprised if we are led astray in many things, and God punishes the blindness of his people as he punished them of old in the exile of Babylon. In this issue, as it stands now before us, not only the moral theology of contraception within marriage but the whole nature of the Church, of the function of the apostolic ministry, of the character and limitation of her teaching authority are at stake. Grave as it may be to write such things, my faith, my conscience and my love for the Church and for the Petrine authority, in which I utterly believe, do not allow me to be silent.

4

The Right to Rule
Recent Developments in the Catholic Church
(1975)

The Roman Catholic Church is, as a straight matter of fact, both Catholic and Roman. It is useful to start by adverting to this duality if we are to understand the nature of recent developments within it.

On the one side there is its wide Catholic character and on the other the undoubtedly strong position of the Roman See within our communion. It would be of course wildly to misunderstand the historical development of the Catholic communion to underestimate the centrality and significance of the position of the See of Rome within it; but, conversely, to concentrate only on what Rome does, or does not do, or orders or doesn't order, to concentrate only on those people who appear most clearly as spokesmen of the See of Rome would be gravely to misunderstand the character of the communion which includes also the Archbishops of Paris, Vienna, Cologne and Madrid and of course sees far, far beyond these. It is extremely important that one doesn't think of it only as being the communion of the See of Rome, and yet of course it is the Roman Communion, which is not the same as the Roman Church. I, for example, am not a member of the Church of Rome, but I am in communion with the Church of Rome, the greatest of churches, the mother of so many saints, whose hospitality moreover I greatly appreciated for several years while I was doing my theological training. My ordination was indeed on the instructions of my own bishop, the Bishop of Masaka, but I was actually ordained by the Vicar General of the Bishop of Rome, Cardinal Micara, some twenty years ago. I am more than happy to have been ordained by the Vicar General of the Bishop of Rome while not belonging to his church, except as a guest. From his communion as a Christian believer I myself could never part. Central to my theme will be the constant interaction of Catholicity and Romanitas in the history of our communion.

Let us start, not in the twentieth century, not the nineteenth, but in the sixteenth. Now the sixteenth century crisis was one, as it seems to me, of three things: doctrine, devotion and institution. There was a clash in all three – the way of teaching; the way of praying; the way of organising the Church. And in all three the Reformation was largely a rebellion in northern Christianity against what we can only call a one-sided Romanisation of the late medieval church.

What we have to face up to across the last ten centuries of Catholic history has been an almost continuous advance in Romanisation. In the fourteenth and fifteenth centuries it was becoming common for bishops to be appointed from Rome, despite the protests of other churches. One sees that beginning already in the thirteenth century, opposed as it was by Grosseteste and others. This was one key area among many in that steady Romanisation of the western church which was destructive of the true Catholicity of diversity between real local churches and productive of a false Catholicity of uniformity: the uniformity of a 'Latin' model. The Reformation was in large part a reaction to this model, a reaction easily linked with political nationalism. The Catholic response to this in the sixteenth century, the response of the counter-Reformation, was quite clearly in part a hardening in defence of precisely those positions which were challenged by Protestants, in particular the organisational position of the Papacy within the church. There was an increased centralisation within the remaining Catholic Communion as a consequence of, and as part of, the counter-Reformation. Yet, at the same time, 'counter-Reformation' is in some ways a very inadequate term to describe that amazing renewal of fervour, of spirituality, of institutional ecclesiastical efficiency, of missionary activity which is what happened in the parts of the Christian church which remained in the communion of Rome in the second part of the sixteenth and the early part of the seventeenth century.

The situation of today is not, however, simply or chiefly a product of the sixteenth century. We know rather that we are heirs, generation after generation, situation after situation, of evolving church history. How decisive then for all our churches was that subsequent stagnation, in some ways not unlike the late medieval stagnation, which went on from the late seventeenth into the early nineteenth century. Again, it was a stagnation, theological, spiritual and institutional which was in many ways common to the Catholic Communion and to the churches which were heirs of the Reformation. But the effect on the Catholic Church lasted longer and went deeper. This was largely due to that very close tie with the absolute monarchies of the Hapsburgs, the Bourbons and their like, and a certain harmony of attitudes which developed between church and state, papacy and monarchy. That harmony was not, I believe, characteristic of the deepest and most authentic political attitude of Catholic Christianity, but it was undoubtedly characteristic of the Catholicism of the period. That epoch of stagnation reached its lowest point in the late eighteenth century with the formal dissolution of the Society of Jesus and the practical dissolution of many other religious orders during the French Revolution and Napoleonic Wars. Seldom did the Catholic Church appear less dynamic, more inert. And yet a vast new move of renewal was about to begin. One can indeed point to many depressing sides of nineteenth century Roman Catholic Christianity, but one must also bear in mind very strongly what a tremendous spiritual revival there was within the Catholic communion from the 1830s on. Think of the vast expansion of the new religious orders and the power of the missionary movement – the emergence in Pio Nono's reign of the White Fathers, the Verona Fathers, the Mill Hill Fathers and the still more numerous wave of sisterhoods: what a tremendous explosion it was in an age not only of missionary foundations but of renewed monastic and contemplative communities too. So many of the great contemplative and scholarly institutions of the modern church do not go back behind the mid-nineteenth century: the time of Dom Guéranger and the foundation of Solesmes, and then of Beuron and Maredsous; Lacordaire's revival of the French Dominicans; the establishment of the Institut Catholique in Paris. So much of modern Catholic Christianity derives its structural form and initial inspiration from the great period of Pius IX. We must not forget this even if we are far from being in sympathy with the political, or the ecclesiastical attitudes of Pius IX. So much was happening in the Catholic Church at that time: it was rather like the later sixteenth century with on the one side a tremendous spiritual, missionary, institutional and even theological renewal, while on the other side there was again a hardening in certain lines, particularly a hardening of centralisation and uniformity. The later nineteenth century undoubtedly saw a new victory for what one can only call the ultramontane and Roman attitude, against the more decentralised Gallican, Cisalpine point of view which was and is still so deeply part of the total Catholic tradition. Those final years of the nineteenth century, the years after the first Vatican Council, the years of modernist crisis and anti-modernist reaction, were a sort of high peak of the ultramontane wave. It is true, yet at the same time, let us not forget that this was the age of Duchesne, of Bremond, of Von Hugel, of Edmund Bishop, of Batiffol, of Blondel and so many other great scholars and spiritual men whom we can look back to. I don't think that men like Von Hugel were only marginal to Catholic life; they were very much part of it. Then too there was the extraordinary missionary expansion of the church in South and North America, in Asia and Africa, the steady multiplication of dioceses from the pontificate of Leo XIII to that of Paul VI. All this was at times assisted, at times frustrated by the steady building up of institutional centralisation, the ever greater stress in many areas of life upon the value of uniformity and of Romanitas.

The trying and difficult period of modernism and anti-modernism was in part left behind after the first world war. I think that if we consider the last forty years as a whole we can see how much of the achievements of Vatican II stem from the 1930s. If one looks at the great prophets of the mid-twentieth century Catholic Church, the prophets — we may say — of the Second Vatican Council — men like Congar, Beauduin, Cardijn, Couturier and many others — they were really doing their best work in the 1930s. They were sowing the seed of which now we may reap the harvest. It is most important that we don't see it all as suddenly coming out of a hat when Pope John arrives. The Vatican Council was in many ways an opening of the door, an opening of the windows to a very deep movement of spiritual, theological, and ecumenical renewal which had been gaining strength for many a year, particularly in the churches of western Europe. If that is so, one might ask "Why was the explosion of Vatican II (in so far as it was an explosion – a controlled explosion) necessary?" It was produced, I think, by accumulated tension between all this growth and renewal upon the one hand, the maintenance of old and rigid institutions (indeed further measures of Roman centralisation) upon the other. The balance within the church between southern Europe and the rest of the world was changing, the balance between laity and clergy, the balance between bishop and theologian. The sheer scale of the Catholic Communion was proving too much for the Roman bureaucrats – and yet they wouldn't give up. So the new realities were coming to clash more and more, not with the basic sense of the Petrine and papal ministry (the need for which is sensed as much as ever) but with the centralising, over-bureaucratic, legalistic, rather bullying character which it has taken on over the centuries – and most of all in the years after the first Vatican Council.

All this was particularly characteristic of the 1950s, the later tired years of Pius XII. At that time I was a student in Rome. We could feel the malaise, and the constant tension between the attitudes of the Curia and Roman officialdom and the new winds now blowing clearly and strongly enough even through one of the most Roman of colleges, my own Propaganda Fide. What the professors were teaching on one side and what we were many of us buying in the college book shop on the other – the works of Congar, De Lubac, and so forth – were very different things. It couldn't have gone on much longer. Pope John had the practical wisdom through which the Holy Spirit could work to open the windows, but it is clear that what happened after Pope John called his Council was not resurgence after decay but an overdue recognition of the vast changes which had been taking place for years in many parts of the Church. Of course, when you officially recognise changes they escalate and at once start to affect even traditional areas hitherto untouched – such as the Roman Catholic Church in this country which, on the whole, had become something of a backwater. A revolutionary movement, even a very peaceful revolutionary movement, cannot stop. Once one point is acquired, another will quite properly be pressed for – something which could not have been feasible to suggest till the first one has been changed. So we should see Pope John's opening of the windows as a response to two things: failure on one side, achievement on the other. Undoubtedly, there has been a long failure in a tight, rather fearful approach to the world, to other churches, to the forward march of the human intellect – an approach which dates partly from the counter-reformation, partly from the nineteenth century, and partly from Pius XII's reign. And the achievement too had its history – in some ways a steady history since the mid-nineteenth century, in others an emergence in the 1930s or a break-through of the post-Second World War period; it was an achievement in lay apostolate (better a deep laicisation of hitherto clerical preserves) in mission and spirituality and theology and liturgy – and parts of it had already been fully approved by Pope Pius XII. Vatican II was to be both a challenge to, and a confirmation of, our recent history.

It is clearly impossible and unnecessary to attempt to outline here the whole history, and the complexity of issues and discussion, of the Second Vatican Council. It raised a diversity of expectations, some fulfilled, many unfulfilled. As for any major event of human history, people saw it at the time, and still see it, from very different points of view. Undoubtedly it triggered off a period of acute ecclesial change not only in our own communion but also in other communions; it would indeed be fascinating to attempt an exact analysis of the effect of the second

Vatican Council on other churches over the last ten years. This wider period of acute ecclesial change is still far from over but to understand it, we can best distinguish the period of the Council and its immediate follow-up from the real post-conciliar period which I conceive as beginning in 1968. In the massive sixteen official documents we find an extremely limited amount of clear practical reform, though many of them do undoubtedly point the way towards the precise, important, fairly limited reforms incorporated in papal directives during the next few years. But behind any immediate practical decisions one sees the much more important deeper doctrinal vision of church, scripture, freedom, the great central themes of the Council – the sort of themes whose implications never can be exhausted. It is important to note, however, that in this vast mass of words there are many passages and even documents which hardly reflect what I would consider the authentic vision of Vatican II at all. You can find whole chunks, which somehow slipped through almost unchanged from the most unsatisfactory of the pre-conciliar drafts, when the greater part of those texts was scrapped. Despite the length of the Council (1962-5) there was a shortage of time, made worse by many of the medieval procedures still insisted upon so that we get some very poor stuff in the final decrees – indeed some are desperately poor as a whole, for example, the decree on Social Communications. So clearly a problem about Vatican II is that you can find almost anything you like in those documents by taking a sentence here, a sentence there, while another person will take something else and offer a quite different stress.

From the viewpoint of other Christians the Decree on Ecumenism is obviously of special importance. It is undoubtedly one of the best documents of the Council, and offers us an ecclesiology of communion, whose implications both theoretical and practical are enormous. 'Communion' is, I am sure, the very best word to use when we speak of what the church is. But hitherto in Catholic doctrine we had really to work with an 'all or nothing' doctrine: either there is 'full communion' and you are in the church, or there is no communion (though perhaps a fruitful 'desire' for it) and you are out. But here instead we find a doctrine of degrees of communion, or partial communion, and of the possibility of quiet growth in communion. This is a true sociological analysis but it is rightly offered as being also a theological one. If we are partly in communion, then we are partly one church – sharing a common baptism though not common bishops. But the sharing can grow, almost organically, (as it can, of course, also diminish); if and as it grows, so too do we become more and more fully 'one church'. This gives the whole ecumenical process a sound theological grounding discovered within central Catholic tradition – and nothing for us can be more important than that. From 'partial communion' we can grow, perhaps almost imperceptibly, into that relationship which Pope Paul has described to the Patriarch of Constantinople as being one of 'almost full communion'. I think that is a tremendously important phrase: almost full. This is such a significantly different vision of the way churches will grow together than anything we had in the past and it is an immensely helpful conciliar contribution. It provides a theological base on which we can work practically and effectively with other churches. At the same time the Council presented a much wider shift in doctrinal and devotional emphasis. Some people feel, and with reason, that the Dogmatic Constitution on Revelation is the most important ecumenical document of the Vatican Council with its forthright statement that the church's 'teaching office is not above the Word of God but serves it'. Again in the Constitution on the Church, *Lumen Gentium,* there is a decisive alteration of balance from the extremely hierarchical, governmental view that we find in the dogmatic theological treatise of the post-Vatican I era to a placing of the primary stress upon the common character of the whole People of God, the Body of Christ, and a firm relegation of any consideration of the hierarchy to Chapter Three. There is also a complete and crucial elimination of the model of 'monarchy' in explaining the role of the Pope. Again, the positioning of the teaching about Mary within the constitution of the church and the whole way that doctrine about Mary is there developed is also of major ecumenical importance. It struck me forcibly when I was studying that final chapter on Mary and looked at the massive footnotes, the references to fathers and theologians, how there is no simple reference to St. Bernard of Clairvaux, St. Alphonsus Liguori or St. Louis-Marie de Montfort, the three writers chiefly responsible for the development of the less restrained type of Catholic Marian devotion. It is, after all, as important to note what was not said as what was said in the documents of the Council.

We come now to the structuring of the church. As I remarked earlier, in the sixteenth century churches divided in three crucial areas: doctrine, devotion and the actual structuring of the church. We have seen too how in subsequent periods there must be recognised a steady further hardening of structure in the direction of centralisation and Roman dominance. Now the greatest single weakness of the Vatican Council, and the source of so many of our problems since, is that the Council shied away from any effective practical approach to the structuring of the Church, though it did doctrinally or theoretically provide ground for a major shift in the practical structuring – a shift away from the tendency of several centuries. It did so by stressing three things. The first of these is the active participation of the laity in the life of the church and this in fact is the one which is coming through most easily: one can think of all sorts of ways, at parish, and diocesan level and in specialist institutions. Secondly, there is the stress upon the collegiality of the bishops. From a doctrinal point of view there can be no doubt that the third chapter of *Lumen Gentium* is extremely important. But it has remained theory rather than practice. Some attempt has been made to realise it through the Synod of Bishops, which has now met five times in Rome. Up till now, I would suggest, the Synod of Bishops has been a failure although not a complete failure. Some of its discussions have been interesting but its decisions remain insignificant. It certainly doesn't respond adequately to a collegial vision of the episcopate. Thirdly, there is what we can best call the re-discovery of the local church in the Second Vatican Council. This always seems to me to have been the most extraordinary thing, for as far as I can see, it was never very strenuously discussed in the debates of the Vatican Council; it just emerged, partly as a pragmatic response to the fact that if you are trying to reform such a vast body as the Catholic Church you simply cannot lay down universally applicable directives in the matter of a pastoral liturgy, the training of priests, or what have you. In area after area the Council Fathers were forced to recognise that the needs of different parts of the world church are so varied that you can only respond to them realistically by giving more authority to the Bishops; you have to recognise the diversity of need in different cultural areas and so the diversity of character between different local churches. From being a practical issue this received theological recognition, but it is one deeply inimical to the Roman mind which has not liked to speak about the 'particular church' (*Ecclesia Particularis*) or about churches in the plural within the communion of the church. So reluctant was it that the phrase does not appear in the constitution on the liturgy published in the second session. That document does not once use the phrase *ecclesia particularis,* the local church, although it is already very largely using the sense, the theology, of the local church. It was very un-

Roman to admit quite explicitly that in the Church there
are churches. In the documents of the third session this
admission was coming through fairly often and if you
count up the number of times in the fourth session documents that we get 'the local church' and even 'the
churches' in the plural it has become very considerable.
Undoubtedly there was a very deep theological shift taking
place at this point through the sessions of the Council, a
shift all the more important in that it never became a
precise issue. It was rather a growth in collective
understanding.

Probably the most important document on this matter
is the Decree on Eastern Catholic Churches, the so-called
Uniates. Here, after all, quite manifestly is a group of local
churches, with their own liturgies, their own canon laws,
their own patterns of church government and so forth, all
different from the Western, Latin Church, though in the
fulness of our communion. Yet we have treated them
pretty poorly. Even in Pope Pius XII's time a uniformity
of western provenance was still being pressed upon them –
modifying their Canon Law, and liturgy. Some of the
points abrogated by the Decree on the Eastern Churches
had only been imposed in 1949 and 1957: let us hope that
they were the very last instances of that steady Latinisa-
tion of Eastern Christian Churches in communion with
Rome which has gone on through the centuries. Certainly,
the Council was anxious to do justice, very generously, to
our Eastern brethren, and it is in that context that we find
what I think is the most important single statement ever
made by the Second Vatican Council. It is in Article 5 of
the Decree on Eastern Churches and runs as follows:
"The Churches of the East, as much as those of the West,
fully enjoy the right and are in duty bound to rule
themselves." I really cannot imagine how this got through
in the strength and the simplicity of the statement. But it

did. Great indeed is the power of the Holy Spirit for here and here alone did the Second Vatican Council declare something 'solemnly' *(sollemniter)*: "This holy Council solemnly declares . . ." it is the only time in the whole of the Council that the word 'solemnly' is used. The Council did not wish to proclaim solemn teaching, yet here perhaps almost unconscious of the vast significance of its words, it did so none the less. The churches of the East, as much as those of the West, have the right and the duty to rule themselves. That means the churches of the West as much as those of the East. Apply that. It is staggeringly opposed to the Romanisation of our communion which we have suffered for too long. How can you rule yourselves if all your bishops are appointed by Rome? Clearly, none of our churches are self-governing.

It is a matter of great interest that very recently the Patriarch of the Maronites died and the Maronites have elected their new Patriarch. This was, of course, in accordance with their perennial custom yet when the last Patriarch died twenty years ago Rome stepped in and appointed his successor. The consequence was almost a schism. At the time it was stated that the Roman intervention was due to particular reasons yet one wondered whether the Maronites were not about to go the way of all our western churches and lose their Canonical freedom of election. As an action it was so clearly in line with the general Roman policy of Pius XII's reign – the steady bringing of the Eastern Churches in line with Western Canonical practice, the pressure to eliminate a married clergy and so forth. However, this time there was not a hint that the Patriarch of the Maronites would be appointed from Rome. He was elected because the Maronites have the right and duty to rule themselves. Here at least a battle has been won.

It remains absurd that we are still speaking or expected to speak in terms of the so-called 'Latin Church' as a unity as if the Church of Italy, the Church of Peru, Australia, Vietnam, Tanzania and everywhere else can be 'the Church of the West', the one Latin Church, while there are twenty other churches in the eastern Mediterranean and southern India. Clearly this is not so. There is no such uniformity. If there is not one 'Church of the East', but many churches, so there is not one Church of the West. There are staggering implications here for the restructuring of the Church but the Council adverted to none of them, yet its teaching on the right to self-government of the local church remains its great time-bomb, bound inevitably to explode sooner or later. Essentially the Catholic Communion is an *ecclesia ecclesiarum,* a Church or communion of Churches, and it is out of that and as a ministerial manifestation of it that we have the collegiality of bishops. In practice it is impossible to have episcopal collegiality if all the bishops in the college are appointed by the head of the college. The bishops are the representatives of their local churches coming together into the college at the same time as they represent the one episcopal College of the *Catholica* to their local churches: their representative character extends both ways. But the reality both of the bishop/college relationship and of the bishop/local church relationship is simply punctured as long as the ancient Catholic tradition of local election is disregarded and replaced by one of nomination by the Roman Curia.

The immediate implementation of the Council's evident wishes took some two years. Up to early 1968 and since that year, we have really entered into a new period. The decisive question that faces us now can be formulated in some such way as this: was Vatican II a set of precise reforms which could be clearly implemented so that we could then come to a full stop; so that we could go through the pages and say, "We have done everything now! Well done, good and faithful servant"? Or was it rather to be seen as a vast vision or, rather, hints towards a new vision of the church, so that written into the most pregnant of its pages, more or less implicitly, there is a programme much more far-reaching, more taxing, more compulsive than anything which was laid down precisely? Did not the key declarations upon freedom, upon the supremacy of scripture, upon the local church, upon ministry as service, have inherent implications for the life of the church which could not be satisfied by the particular and rather bureaucratic reforms envisaged by the majority of the Council Fathers and since carried out so dutifully by Pope Paul? No man can see all the implications, or the most important implications, of sudden deep and decisive insights of this sort. What we are doing, and compelled to do during this new period, is to wrestle with the deeper consequences for church life of the sort of commitment to Word and world which the Fathers of Vatican II unwarily accepted. It is proving very hard.

Lumen Gentium, Vatican II's Constitution on the Church, offers a vision of the Church which is widely different from that provided by the official theological treatises of the first half of the twentieth century. Pope Pius XII's papacy operated in accordance with those treatises; hence if there has been no major change in operation of the papacy after Vatican II from the practice of Pius XII it is certain that today's papal practice is not in accordance with conciliar theory. Theory is indeed sometimes much easier to change than practice. Papal practice has admittedly significantly changed – the episcopal synods, a considerable internationalisation of the Curia, the abolition of the Index, and so forth. One can point to many things. But must one not admit that their significance is still marginal? The essential questions of centralisation, Romanisation, the control of power have not been faced. Indeed one could argue quite effectively that there has been a considerable move into further centralisation, particularly in strengthening the control of the Secretariat of State, subordinating to it even the different departments in the Curia which had up to now a rather healthy independence. In the last ten years the Secretariat of State has come out more than ever on top; it has grown considerably in size and personnel in the Vatican and abroad, achieving a further centralisation of ecclesiastical power of a bureacratic kind precisely since the Council. Has not the Papacy to function in a qualitatively different manner if one is to take *Lumen Gentium,* collegiality, the local church, and so much else seriously? This is the basic issue which underlies all the particular crises and questions which were largely shelved in Vatican II, things like the morality of forms of birth control, compulsory celibacy for all priests, the manner of choosing bishops, the shape of the liturgy, the possiblity of intercommunion. Our problems are made worse (as they were in the mid-1950s, the last years of Pius XII) by the difficulty of an ageing Pope. Pope Paul's supreme achievement was to carry Pope John's Council through with great patience and effectiveness and to ensure in a very gentle manner that the immediate tensions of the Council and subsequent years were contained without schism. The last eight years have not been good ones for institutional leadership of any sort in this world. In retrospect Pope Paul may be judged to have done far better than his contemporaries: Pope John's contemporaries were Kennedy and Macmillan, Pope Paul's Nixon and Heath! It is an age of bewilderment and cynicism in which little mercy is shown to the leader who fails to turn up trumps every time. But undoubtedly the Pope is now an old man, closely surrounded by curial officials determined to keep Rome running the way it was. One senses a growing gap between the reality of what is happening in the wider church and the mind and statements of the Pope tragically dissuaded from retiring.

Now more than ever the Catholic Church is not Rome.

If one looked only or chiefly at Rome one could take a very pessimistic view of the contemporary church and not see the growth, the vitality, the waves of renewal which go on and on – in Africa and South America, in Spain and in India, in this country too. If confidence in the leadership is lower than it has been for a long time, the laity at least may have more confidence than previously in themselves and in the Holy Spirit: unsure of all things, but not unsure of God.

Yes, we are unsure of many things. Priests leave, and fewer are ordained. Religious houses close. The bishops offer a leadership as banal as it is ineffective. The confident co-operation of bishops and theologians which was such a striking characteristic of the Council years has been almost wholly lost, and yet there are continually new initiatives in lay prayer, community and ministry and in the field of inter-Christian co-operation: local sharing of work and worship between Roman Catholics and other Christians has grown immensely in this country even since 1970. The truth is that we lived for long in a far too clerically controlled church; today the clerical controls are in large part simply fading away. Undoubtedly an immediate cause is a sheer weakening in the number and calibre of the clergy, but loss can also be great gain. The Catholic Church of the future will be, beyond all imagining, a lay church even if for some years it still puts up, ever so politely, with residual clerical pockets unable to understand the new order.

Clergy/laity, Rome/local church – these are the two hubs of our creative discontent. In this country more than most it will still take some time to get away from the pattern of the clerically controlled and ultramontane church we have taken for granted since the mid-nineteenth century, but it is coming even here. In the meantime the natural conservatism of bishops, priests and laity is very understandable. Under the shadow of Manning and his friends men were trained one way and cannot be retrained in a day. Certainly there has been some basic failure on the part of our leadership to understand the principles actually annunciated by Vatican II at their most creative and most significant levels in regard to the structure of the church and human freedom. Here, as so many times in the past, we are still faced with two basically conflicting models: the Roman, uniform, governmentally controlled church on the one hand and a diversity of local churches within the fullness of the Catholic communion of the people of God on the other. It would, doubtless, be idle to imagine that here at the crucial point of centuries of Roman development some statements of a single council, quite inadequately grasped in their real meaning by most of the council members and quite unprovided with structural implementation by the council, could suffice to change the course of the Roman juggernaut or persuade the Curia to alter its ways. Yet it is here that the battle is being fought and has to be fought – and primarily by those within the Catholic communion. The battle is not, of course, to eliminate the Petrine ministry but to recreate in hard practice a balance between centre and local church, between hierarch and prophet, between clergy and laity. And this is being fought, painfully and with difficulty. It is being fought by those who stand and go on fighting.

I would sense that if this is the central problem of our own communion, it is also where the gordian knot of the ecumenical dilemma is to be found. I would think that more and more between Roman Catholics and Anglicans there is the growing consciousness of an adequate degree of doctrinal unity in the areas of our central concern; this is made possible partly by a much greater realisation that considerable theological, pastoral and devotional differences can be catered for within the pluralism, the comprehensiveness proper to the true church and to a single communion. If there are beliefs and practices of some seriousness upon one side or another, of which others quite clearly do not approve, these diversities can often rightly be tolerated within this comprehensiveness. The recognition of the possibility of a creative comprehensiveness within unity is allowing individuals and groups at local level to go forward in a measure of understanding to a sharing of mission such that the division of communion appears today increasingly anachronistic and pointlessly painful. But, as I say, there is a gordian knot which comes from the centralised institutional lack of change within the Roman Catholic communion: the Roman refusal to alter significantly its understanding and practice of the institutional implications of Petrine ministry. The very same blockage which is at the heart of the crises within our own communion in the last few years is also at the heart of a blockage with regard to real ecumenical progress.

To put it bluntly, there can be no feasible pattern of organic or institutional unity between the See of Rome and the See of Canterbury, while no pattern is admitted providing a similar independence for the See of Westminster and all that it stands for. There is, after all, already an *Ecclesia Anglicana* in communion with the See of Rome – I am a member of it and the Cardinal is its senior bishop – but it is a local church in bondage, unable to choose its own bishops, being perpetually ordered about from Rome to do this or that – even to unify the English form of its own liturgy and much else. Only when Westminster is free – when to it has been applied in all sincerity that solemn declaration of Article 5 of the Decree on Eastern Catholic Churches – is it feasible to think of Canterbury returning into the fullness of Catholic communion; but then, of course, there will be no continued need for the duality of Westminster and Canterbury, and we English language Catholics of the Roman communion will be able joyfully to return to the flock of the mother church of the English speaking peoples, from which only our loyalty to the Petrine ministry and the breadth of Catholic communion has for so long sorrowfully severed us.

5

The Right to Celebrate
Sharing the cup

When I came to Aberdeen in September 1976 I found myself not permitted to give communion of the cup to the laity even at ordinary weekday masses. To do so had become for me very much a matter of principle. Celebrating Mass means celebrating in a human way (though vastly more so) and this involves the sharing together of food and drink. Truncate the sharing and you truncate the celebration itself. It remains a valid mass but not, sacramentally, a celebration. After some months I decided I could not go on administering the sacrament in a way I found, quite simply, wrong. I thought it would be far more fruitful to make a public protest and I produced the statement which follows and which appeared in The Tablet of 26 February 1977. For me it was, and remains, a very important statement and something of a watershed in my priestly life. It is all the more necessary and encouraging to add that in Aberdeen itself just one year later things are now very different. In the university chaplaincy the cup is given to the laity at every mass and the new bishop is encouraging communion in both kinds for many occasions throughout the diocese. The renewal for which he is struggling so zealously is one among many examples of the pastoral vitality the Catholic Church continues to show today. This does not convince me that I should not have made my stand or should not do so again over other matters. On the contrary, it convinces me that my gesture was well worth while, indeed overdue, but only part, just one very little part, of the ongoing processes of a very odd, infuriating, but still beloved body.

*At the end of last year (1976) I took the decision not to preside or concelebrate at Mass in future when the cup is not offered to the laity, unless there are present social circumstances to justify that exclusion on a particular occasion, such as a very large congregation.

To explain this very serious decision, over a matter which has for many years exercised me greatly I can best begin by quoting what I wrote nine years ago in *A Concise Guide to the Documents of the Second Vatican Council* (1968), volume 1, page 131: "If the body of Christ is linked in a particular way with the idea of incorporation into the mystical body the blood of Christ is connected specially with the idea of the new covenant and membership of the new people of God. Both apply equally to the laity. Now that the Canon is to be said in the vernacular, it becomes still more false and frustrating to

*The text which follows first appeared on 26th February 1977 in *The Tablet* under the following editor's rubric: "This personal statement is published in deference to the earnest request of a valued contributor and friend. Ed."

refuse the cup to the laity just after recalling in a loud voice Christ's own words: "Drink of it, all of you." This is the most solemn command our Master ever gave us – his final memorial before his death. If the conciliar statement that the Church's "teaching office is not above the word of God, but serves it" (*Dogmatic Constitution on Revelation,* Art. 10) has any meaning at all, it must be applied here and should have been all along. The total exclusion of the laity from the chalice is indefensible on sound principles, and we must have the honesty to admit it. Today, in this, as in other matters, the council is leading us back to authentic tradition, and that incidentally means coming closer to other Christians too."

For some five years up to last summer I served or worshipped in Britain in churches where this sound principle was admitted, at least in large part – the university chaplaincies of Birmingham and Cambridge, St. Edmund's House at Cambridge, St. Margaret's parish in Twickenham, and various monasteries and convents. Progress might be slow and limited in this as in other fields, but there was enough of it to permit patience without forcing one into a pattern of sacramental behaviour which one had come to believe wrong in itself and in conflict with the finest insights of the council. To go back today to square one because one has moved to a more conservative part of the Church I find morally impossible: one is forced on the contrary to clarify one's own position. As this is not of its nature a private matter but a very public one, indeed one absolutely central to an ordained priest's most clearly specified function, and as the partial withdrawal from the exercise of that function is itself a decision with clear public implications, and one in which his own reputation is undoubtedly involved, a priest cannot but feel bound to make public the reasoning behind such a decision.

Eleven years after the council I think it is not precipitate to claim that communion of the cup should now be free for all who so desire, and that it is indeed intolerable to find any part of the Catholic Church where so simple an obedience to the direct words of Jesus, words treasured by the Church through the ages and daily repeated by priests, is actually forbidden and strictly forbidden by authority.

I can see practical problems in the universal sharing of the cup in places where churches are very poor and congregations very large, though I suspect they can still be overcome. I can see no conceivable justification in Britain for not making communion in both kinds the norm for all who so desire in weekday Masses everywhere and for Sunday Masses at least in university chaplaincies and many similar congregations.

I find that many priests and lay people judge my concern over this as odd or at least exaggerated, and behind this reaction I sense a deeper disagreement as to how one finally sees the Mass. For many people who greatly value it, its form is really a matter of very little significance. What matters is an objective action, generally expressed in terms of sacrifice. While I would not for a moment deny the objective and sacrificial character of the Eucharist, I see the total meaning of this central sacrament as vastly wider than that and I believe that its celebration in a seriously defective way can be so misleading and painful that it becomes better to withdraw from the enacting of what is still "valid" than to participate in the systematic forming of wrong attitudes or, equally the turning away of people – especially young people – by a pattern of behaviour which appears contradictory to the true meaning of the Eucharist or to an aspect of that meaning which deserves particular emphasis at the present time.

The Vatican Council stressed again and again that the Eucharist is the "sacrament of unity" and as such the focal point of the people of God, itself a sacrament of unity. The Council described the Mass as "the pre-eminent manifestation of the Church" (*Liturgy*, Art. 41), and the central principle of its liturgical reforms was that the rites should "clearly express the holy things they signify" (Art. 21). Now one of the chief "holy things" which the Mass signifies is indeed the *koinonia*, the fellowship, of Christians in Christ which is most clearly expressed by the symbol of the common cup. A systematic denial of the cup to the laity is, I believe, profoundly opposed to all that Vatican II was centrally concerned with, and its implications have a crushing importance not only for the liturgy but also for the pastoral and catechetical message our times need. It does not surprise me if a church, which systematically refuses to accept this central symbol of *koinonia* generously, simply loses its young people, and I believe that it deserves to do so. The form of the central sacrament determines the whole ethos of a church and its message. Personally I find myself psychologically incapable of preaching about almost any aspect of the *koinonia* of Christian life if I am at the same time identified with a denial of the sacramental *koinonia* of the cup.

So this is not primarily a matter of rubrics nor of ecumenism, not of conformity to the guidance of the Vatican Council or some other recent ecclesiastical document. It is in my view a matter of basic ecclesial and priestly integrity which can either be expressed at the most solemn moment of our worship, faith and communion, or is denied through the maintenance of a pattern of clerical privilege derived from the close of the Middle Ages. The priest says before the whole congregation: "Drink of this, all of you"; he adds a little later, according to the new eucharistic prayers: "May all of us who share in the body and blood of Christ be brought together in unity", "Grant that we, who are nourished by his body and blood, may be filled with his Holy Spirit," or "gather all who share this one bread and one cup into the one body of Christ". He then proceeds to drink the cup himself alone or to share it with a concelebrant while offering the lay people present (perhaps, in a weekday Mass, just two or three) only bread. The sacrament of obedience to Christ, of shared love and fellowship, is therefore twisted into somehow expressing clerical apartness and a certain disregard for what Christ actually asked us to do: it even hints at the power of the man in authority to create a sphere of privilege with its own special perks and so exclude common folk from the fullness of life. This may sound very unfair, and I fully agree that these are not the conscious motives of priests who do not give the cup today, nor do they explain the largely accidental process whereby centuries ago communion in one kind became normative in the western Church – though it certainly did happen against a background of the increasing overall clericalisation of the Church. But they do, I believe, indicate fairly enough the objective sociological sense of the practice of excluding the laity from communion of the cup, except for rare privileged occasions, in modern times. That exclusion, at least in smaller groups, strikes harshly counter to the wider message one is fumbling to proclaim or, rather, to let the Eucharist itself proclaim through the manifest power of its celebration.

It is my conviction that there is nothing more important for the Church than the demonstration of integrity and there is nothing which renders it more lacking in credibility in today's world than an institutionalised gap between ecclesial praxis and ecclesial teaching, between deed and word. Such a failure has here been ritualised at the most sensitive point of our following of Christ, and I can stand it no more. As I grow older and more conscious of the very little power I have to change anything, I become more resolved to rescue at least my personal life from the clericalism which has hitherto so greatly bound both it and that of the whole Church.

With communion of the cup goes the far lesser matter of giving communion in the hand to all those who prefer it. Here too, if in a smaller way, a hard authoritarian maintenance of a clericalist structure for the Eucharist – sharply differentiating the way the laity receive from the way the clergy do – both disfigures the full meaning of the sacrament and is, I am sure, wholly at variance with the sort of ministry the Church needs today and will need still more tomorrow. Many priests and lay people may reasonably feel that these points are secondary in their list of priorities, and if a reasonable freedom be allowed in this field then I would agree. But the exclusion of freedom forces one to take up a harder line than one would otherwise wish – and it is a painful line for a person to take who after 21 years of ministry has remained (or perhaps even grown) profoundly Mass centred. But I have honestly to admit that I would now prefer not to say Mass than to say it while systematically refusing the cup to the laity with whom I am "celebrating."

6

The Triangle of Salvation

Christian faith convinces us that Jesus of Nazareth is the embodiment and manifestation of God's love for men in a way at once unique and exemplific: divine love revealed and shared in human life; human life so tempered, so transfigured in a yet continuingly human way that it points towards, makes somehow present, draws one to enter into, divine life. He did this by conversation, friendship, a way of life and a way of death, the continual implications of all he said and did. Within the multiplicity of word and action, much of it apparently trivial and indeed necessarily trivial, he convinced the world of love — that God does love and man can love, that love can drive out sin and fear and suffering and even death, that love works forgiveness, that love justifies; that God is love and does forgive, that in Christ indeed he has forgiven; that love overcomes. This communication of divinity, this making of victorious love really and credibly present, was done through three inter-involved channels: the friendship and fellowship of his company, *koinonia*; the message he proclaimed, the *kerygma* of his word; the service to those in affliction he continually gave, the *diakonia* of response to immediate human need. All this was of course made infinitely more compelling, decisive, poignant and precise by his passion, death and resurrection. But these could hardly have a communicable meaning were it not for the preceding and more humanly comprehensible outpouring of koinonia, kergyma and diakonia in the public life of Jesus to all of which the cross was indeed his own great amen, and such an amen that henceforth word, service and fellowship would all have it at their very heart as they flow out in the power and certainty of the resurrection.

Such was the life and mission of Jesus: an approach to his fellow men in which these three strands were inextricably interwoven, in which each utterly presupposed the other two, and in which all three both incarnated and pointed to the reality, the sufficiency, the plenitude, the superabundance, the invincibility of divine love.

The disciple should be as his master; the task passed on is the master's mission; Jesus' life is nothing if not an example. Christian life will then necessarily be christian mission, and christian mission will be neither more nor less nor other than the responsibility to partake in, embody and manifest the divine love revealed by Jesus through a continual process of shared fellowship, uttering a message, providing a service. Not just one or another, but all three. Maybe indeed the degree of embodiment and manifestation of God's love possible by sinful human beings can never be more than the merest whisper and hint of the reality, yet it is the conviction of christian faith that this mere whisper and hint remain of supreme importance, immensely potent, comforting and liberating.

Mission means sending, and there is a sequence of sending within the economy of redemption: the sending of Jesus Christ, the supreme 'Apostle' (Heb. 3:1), by the

Father; the sending of the Holy Spirit; the original sending of men by Christ both during his earthly life and in the post-resurrection appearances; the subsequent and renewed sending of men in every century in the name of Christ by the power of the Spirit. In a Catholic and evangelical view of the church we are as church not only a community of those to whom something has been sent, of those who have received the person and the message sent, but equally a community of the sent: not only possessors of the gifts of Christ, the word, grace, love, hope, but co-givers, co-workers, fellow apostles. Indeed it is because we really are sent in the very same instant as we are found – the gift of justifying grace making us at once partners in the very action of the mystery of Christ – that we are a community at all: a proclaiming community, a church of the sent, a missionary fellowship in the world to manifest the love and truth of God. Mission is then as fundamental as church.

Mission generates communion: it brings men into *koinonia*, that fellowship of love, of union with Father, Son, Spirit and brethren which is the very essence of what we mean by church and the life of grace. Mission continually brings men into fellowship, but fellowship equally continually thrusts outward, generating further witness and service. The mission is *'koinonial'*, the church is confessing.

Jesus Christ was himself the apostle, nor merely by commission, but by his whole being, sense of purpose and behaviour: he manifested, he proclaimed, he somehow enacted God. He was in fact the sacrament of God to the world – showing in worldly terms what God means, making God present, pointing to God still incomprehensibly transcendent. A sacrament is an earthly thing, visible, touchable, at first sight essentially commonplace, clearly remaining itself and yet equally decisively pointing to and presenting something of quite another order. Its use appears profoundly characteristic of the divine economy as christian understanding finds it to be. So much is this the case, that it seems proper to describe Christ himself by this term. *Par excellence* he is sacrament – the sacrament of God, of divine love and the life that this signifies for men. He was such by his very being, but one could not see his inner being or as such comprehend it. What one could see and hear and, at least to some extent, comprehend were his words and actions. By his teaching, his curing, the immediate freeing effected by a relationship with him, by the admittedly and necessarily limited possibilities of participation in his company, he was the sacrament of an unlimited love, an unlimited freedom, an unlimited enrichment. Somehow these things were real and present in him.

The Second Vatican Council has repeatedly recalled the truth that the church, the body of Christ, has itself this same character (*Lumen Gentium,* 1, 9, 48. *Sacrosanctum Concilium,* 26. *Gaudium et Spes,* 42, 45. *Ad Gentes,* 1): it is and must be the sign of Christ, sharing his sacramental nature, pointing towards and making present the truth and love of God which – when participated in by men – already constitute a real beginning to the life and fellowship of the Kingdom. It is the sacrament of salvation. Yet like Christ, the church will be sacrament not just by the abstract depths of its 'essence' and constitution, but by the total complex of its observable structures and behaviour. A sacrament is nothing if not observable, but it impinges upon the observer at two levels, consisting as it does of both matter and form; on one side water, bread, the laying on of hands by one man upon the head of another; on the other side words of interpretation which make this pouring of water, this piece of bread, this manual action different from others, which give to them a vastly heightened meaning, making present through something commonplace a new and revelatory order of things. Natural, human reality and a word of interpretation –

matter and form as we are accustomed to call them — these combined together and not separately, constitute a sacrament. Such is the eucharist and baptism; such too is Christ; such is the church. The bread is not different from other bread, the water from other water; friendship, service, self-sacrifice, dying for others, these are not as such different even in the life of Christ or in that of the church from what can be found elsewhere in human living. What as such is different is the interpretative word.

It is often asked these days: what, if anything, is specific in the sort of service and temporal assistance that Christians offer? How does it differ from that of humanists? Can Christians contribute something in the field of human and social development which non-Christians simply could not? The answer at the level of the actual work done, the sick man tended, the irrigation ditches dug, the co-operative organised, a corrupt and tyrannical government exposed (all belong to the "matter" which makes up the sacrament of christian life) is, and must be, decidedly 'no'. It cannot be. But equally at the level of their deeper interpreted significance in human life — the level of 'form' — the answer is, and must be, 'yes'.

The church as a sign to the world, as a missionary community, as mission, can only approach the world as Christ approached it: as a human presence, a fellowship; as the offer of service, responding to man's needs of here and now; and then, across these first two, as an affirmation, sometimes so gentle sometimes strident of a divine message of revelation, redemption and reconciliation; and all these signifying love. A fellowship, then, with a message — the *kergyma*; with a task of helpfulness — the *diakonia*. The nature of our task is to be found, I believe, in the authenticity of each of these two, integrated and interacting as matter and form of the sacrament of being church-on-mission. But if diakonia is the matter and kerygma the form, what then are we to say about koinonia, the fellowship itself? The answer is that diakonia and kerygma are meaningless apart from the communion. The diakonia of the church is always in reality a koinonial diakonia – service by the fellowship, in the spirit of fellowship, leading into fellowship. Equally kerygma is not primarily a matter of books or radio, it is as such a human reality but not an individualistic reality, it is the message of a believing fellowship. It is a koinonial kerygma. Hence the matter of the sacrament of the church should be seen as the fellowship in service; the diakonal koinonia. The form of the sacrament is the fellowship testifying: the kerygmatic koinonia.

Both diakonia and kerygma mean liberation. This is the very heart of the 'Evangelium', the good news of salvation: Christ came as a redeemer and liberator. He came to free the whole man, and it was across immediate temporal secular liberations that he pointed and we can point to the ultimate liberation of the Gospel. Thus it had been from the beginning. The primary biblical concept of salvation had always been one of God delivering his people from temporal pressures. He rescued them from the tyranny of Egypt, he gave them a land of their own where they would be free, properly fed, able to develop their own culture and to hear him through their own national development. It was in the hard terms of Exodus, of an immediate political liberation, that God chose to express a liberation which is finally found to be much more than political, more than temporal, which is ultimate. 'I have seen the affliction of my people . . . have heard their cry because of their task masters; and I have come to deliver them.' (Ex. 3:30). Even at the time, Moses 'interpreted' the deliverance from Egypt in terms of a vastly more far-reaching covenant of salvation, and the paschal mystery of the new alliance represents a still further interpretation and universalisation of the Exodus deliverance, which from being a particular event has come to express a permanent pattern in God's action on his people. If one is to adhere to this catechesis of the Bible, which is indeed far more than catechesis, then any post-immediate salvation has somehow to be shown to grow out of, to be an added dimension to, deliverance from the immediate fear and need: whether it be of the people as a whole, whether it be of a class or of an individual pressed upon by society, hard circumstances or agony of spirit.

What was true of the Old Testament is also profoundly true of the New. It provides no ground for a field of religious deliverance separated from that of secular deliverance. The gospel of the Kingdom was manifested by Christ with urgency, with repetition and with great clarity within a pattern of predominantly this-worldly liberation – from the slavery of being deaf, dumb, blind, paralytic. 'The Spirit of the Lord is upon me', Christ proclaimed at the beginning of his ministry, 'to announce good news to the poor, to proclaim release for prisoners.' (Lk 4:18). 'Go and tell John what you hear and see: the blind recover their sight, the lame walk, the lepers are cleansed, the deaf hear, the dead are raised to life, the poor are hearing the good news.' (Mt 11:4). Only in terms of immediate secular deliverance was it possible to point towards ultimate deliverance, and 'salvation' as an already experienceable reality emphatically includes both. This is the context, and the only possible context, in which to proclaim the full gospel. And the proof that the gospel is authentically accepted by any man is of the same order again – evidence of personal participation in the struggle for temporal liberation: 'I was hungry and you gave me food: thirsty, you gave me drink; when I was a stranger you took me into your home, when naked you clothed me; when I was ill you came to my help, when in prison you visited me.' (Mt 25:35-36).

The kerygma is the Gospel of ultimate deliverance; its vehicle and immediate actualisation, without which the kerygmatic Word remains essentially inauthentic, is the diakonia of immediate secular deliverance. The latter is the sacrament of the former, or shall we say it provides the matter for which the Gospel gives the interpretative norm. The latter takes the temporal needs of men – escape from Egypt, from leprosy, from poverty and ignorance, from racial tyranny – and through it reveals a deliverance which goes far beyond the immediate need. But this ultimate deliverance cannot in a world of space and time meaningfully actualise itself except sacramentally across immediate deliverance. Hence it is the prime duty of the bearer of the message of ultimate deliverance to provide it with an adequate, a here and now relevant vehicle of secular significance. A Gospel which is not so actualised in terms of temporal liberation, but is used instead as a substitute for the latter, is a bogus message, the opium of the people in the classical sense. The religion of the Incarnate Word requires that, just as the ultimate word only comes to men across limited human words fully participating in the historicity of this world, so ultimate redemption comes to us and makes sense across limited redemptions fully partaking of the materiality and historicity of temporal life. To preach redemption in any other way is not to preach the redemption of the Incarnate Word.

None of this is new. Secular concern has always been recognised as a decisive mark of the true Christian. The church's long record of diakonia is as indisputable as her record of kerygma, though the theology behind it has been far less articulated. Certainly in century after century there has been a tendency within the church to make of secular concern a matter of somewhat marginal importance, quite secondary both to preparation for the 'other world' and to building up a specifically ecclesiastical order in this one, a succumbing to the temptation to let the church retreat into its own circle, creating a pseudo-world of religious validity; but in every age too the church has been called back from this, and it is the function of prophets so to do. In doing so they may have to struggle for the purity of both kerygma and diakonia even against their normal ministers.

Diakonia, like kerygma, must certainly take on many institutional forms, while escaping the death-grip of total institutionalisation. Without systems and institutions man's needs can seldom be met, and the diakonia of the church would not be properly human, not basically incarnate, if it spurned the discipline of the permanent ordered structure. Yet structures not only serve, but can subtly control and falsify the very thrust of a work. An institute founded to serve the poor, to manifest diakonia within an area of undoubted need, manages to develop over the years into a very different thing, becoming another comfortable case of care by the 'haves' for the 'haves'; it comes indeed to under-gird, instead of challenging, their very quality of 'have-ness'. To how many religious institutions and monasteries has this not happened! It is too often subsequently justified either by the requirements of a rather literal fidelity to instructions of another age, or quite simply by the need to obtain sufficient money to go on maintaining themselves and their stately buildings.

The church cannot for a moment abandon the kerygma; if she has any final justification to exist, it is that she has a word to proclaim, a revealed word, an infinitely precious word. In the depths of her being she *is* kerygma. Her whole being is one of proclamation. If she were silent she would not be the church. But it is not her own word; it is the word of God, and a word for the world, a word for everyman. The word of the Son, of cross and resurrection, is too precious for humanity as such that its bearer could possibly be considered excused from proclaiming to some peoples or in some places or cultures. It is the utterly unavoidable obligation of the *Catholica* to proclaim the New Adam and to interpret all human life in the terms of the Incarnate Son of God *per orbem terrarum.*

This kerygma is always a diakonal kerygma, for the word the church is proclaiming is that of the suffering servant, the Christ who came to serve, not to be served. The kerygma is a message whose implications go far beyond immediate society, promising a fullness of liberation neither attainable nor imaginable in our present world, but it is not a message which detaches itself from this society. Vis-à-vis individual things it is a message of detachment, but vis-à-vis the world as such, that is to say the society of man, it is not a message of detachment but of involvement and of concern – a concern for the whole of created manhood, all men and in their wholeness. It is such a burning concern for the things that really matter that it does indeed produce rare detachment from the minor petty comforts that can loom so large in a privatised life. But to seek for a 'pure gospel', a gospel without a continual diakonal character, a gospel not incarnated in the block of personal, social, economic and political reality is to seek for a pseudo-gospel. The Magnificat verse: "He has put down the mighty and raised up the lowly", the statement that "a man's life does not consist in building up a superfluity of possessions," the Judgement criteria of Matthew 25, the programme enunciated in the synagogue at Nazareth, the parable of the Good Samaritan, the sheer fact of the miracles of healing, the whole of the epistle of St. James – all these are not only invitations to diakonia, but they are an absolutely essential element in the kerygma. The kerygma is necessarily diakonal.

It is indeed intrinsically diakonal. While it continually sprouts new forms of diakonia, its mere presence in its purest form is most deeply diakonal. By the sheer power of being itself it liberates, it judges, it reassures, it rejuvenates. When adversity of circumstances makes any other diakonia next to impossible, then indeed does the gospel stand forth most clearly as diakonal. For the man alone and dying, to whom no other diakonia can be or is offered the kerygma is liberation and not opium – not only future liberation but present liberation. Stripped of every other consequence, in this lone moment of time, the diakonal quality of the kerygma – of Christ crucified and risen – is without parallel.

The church is diakonia. This is not just one of a number of things to be applied adjectively, it is a substantive predicate, and the church is still most authentically church when it is not explicitly proclaiming at all, so long as it is serving, and such it has always been. It is service, of the whole man and as whole: mind and body according to his needs of here and now, his real needs, not some imagined ones. Because men are social beings, political beings, economic beings, so diakonia, the daily work of temporal liberation, has to have social, political and economic dimensions. Man, says Aristotle, is a political animal; to treat him otherwise is to reduce him to a vegetable. To imagine that you can authentically serve man while abstracting from this essential of his being is a nonsense. The freeing of man from the present servitude is not only a freeing from hunger and illiteracy and leprosy, it is also and indeed more eminently – for these are deeper, more moral evils – a freeing from man's oppression of man, from the humiliation of second-class citizenship, from expulsion from the place of one's birth, from the insult of 'Whites only'.

All men are in need of liberation, are waiting for diakonia: this includes those dedicated to the liberation of others; and those who by their actions, institutions, status or merely complacency, effectively impede the liberation of others. The pressures of modern affluent society, of boredom, of drugs, of mindless employment, the fear of death and so much else may be just as oppressive, and may require just as much liberation as many pressures which are directly political and economic. Christian *diakonia* is concerned with them all. Moreover, the pressures of over-privilege are at least as humanly destructive as the pressures of political under-privilege: not only the tyrannised but the tyrant is in need of diakonia as much as of kerygma, but his too must be a diakonia which challenges his state not comforts him within it, and which does not approach him by condoning, or seemingly identifying the church with, his political tyranny over others.

Diakonal liberation struggles to free man from the causes of fear. When however the causes cannot be removed, it will indeed endeavour to overcome fear even while the causes remain; it will help man to be a liberated man thriving within an unliberated situation – and such indeed we have all to be – but it has to do this without in any way condoning the causes of unfreedom or denying its responsibility to battle with them as it may.

This diakonia is always a kerygmatic diakonia. The service given flows out from a judgement in faith, the active response to an over-all interpretation of life. It is a service which, faced with the multiple needs and pressures of human society, can weigh them up according to the spirit of Christ, a service which by its priorities and its character proclaims the gospel even when no word at all is said; indeed it may then be at its most intensely kerygmatic – the sheer quality of service must proclaim most incontrovertibly the mysteries of human solidarity and the invincibility of love, human and divine. It is a service whose absolute unavoidability derives from faith, from the acceptance of God's word as to what sort of a thing man is and of what God wants of man. It is service in terms of Christ, a service which imitates Christ, seeks Christ, finds Christ. A service which is Christ being served and Christ serving.

The kerygma interprets both the diakonia and the human experience to which the diakonia responds. Indeed the liberating and therapeutic value of christian diakonia must depend in great part upon the truth of its kerygmatic interpretative matrix. It is clear that any form of human service must carry with it and presuppose some measure of interpretation of human experience, some being more adequate than others. And the christian kerygma too, as interpreter both of the human predicament and of the diakonia, can vary in quality in different historic situations being either more or less adequate, more or less authentic and consistent with its own deepest self. Just as the diakonia offered by Christians may at times be in fact ill-judged, ill-adapted to true immediate needs, so the kerygma that goes with it may be a mis-shapen and largely inauthentic kerygma. The living church at any given historical moment will certainly be uttering a kerygma, and that kerygma cannot be wholly other than the very kerygma of Christ, but it may be considerably so – it may be so overstressing some elements, so silent about others that the kerygma offered here and now must be accounted a corrupt kerygma. Equally the living church always offers diakonia but at times and places this may be largely – though never wholly – an irrelevant, futile, even oppressive diakonia. In so far as the church does this, it is corrupt; and the church is always partially corrupt, though never wholly so.

It remains true none the less that christian kerygma in so far as it is fully itself is the only adequate interpretative matrix for the totality of human experience, and therefore also that true christian diakonia which springs from such an interpretation is also the most thoroughly liberating of any human activity.

Both kerygma and diakonia are at once personal and communal. A message and a service to each individual but also a message and service to the world. The church is the community of men reformed. Her message is a message for society, not merely a message to the single soul, and so also her diakonia has to be a communal diakonia, because hers is a message and a service in terms of Christ the new Adam, the form of a renewed society.

Kerygma and diakonia have, again, to be related to the possible and to the preferable within a given situation. Some things are quite impossible in one situation, possible in another – explicit proclamation is not possible today in Afghanistan, it is in Indonesia; coping with large scale malnutrition was not possible in Africa at the beginning of this century, today it is. Within the possible there is a vast range of alternatives, and no decisive guideline to tell one which to choose. Much will depend here on the prudent judgement of the individual or group, much too on the personal sense of charism, vocation, a frank division of tasks. Some Christians will feel the call to offer much explicit witness, to be evangelists in the strict sense, but many more will carry the priceless burden of a silent kerygma all their lives with little more than the implicit message behind the service of their neighbours and their calm and cheerfulness, the occasional quiet chat, the teaching of their children. Those who feel the call to full-time missionary work of a professional kind have still to decide whether to concentrate upon a kerygma such that it must then generate diakonia, or upon a diakonia such that it cannot but imply a message of salvation. Wise men will relate the use of their energies to the possibilities and priorities inherent within the contemporary situation, while recognising that each man has his own way and that there is no absolute standard as to what in the concrete situation it is most important to do. At a personal level what is both possible and even requisite for one may be quite out of the possible for another.

If each Christian is called to an inescapable responsibility of personal witness, the church is all the same a community and her mission is a communal responsibility. As she is called to a communal kerygma, so is she called to a communal diakonia. And this too we can see from church history to have been a constantly recognised fact. Time after time we see how the church has been galvanised by movements of one kind and another, frequently through the founding of new religious orders, to new and contemporary responses of communal diakonia. What is often impossible for the individual to achieve can be managed by a group, and it is above all as a group, as the body of Christ in the world, that we have to manifest Christ's concern for the hungry, the needy, the depressed, the oppressed – all those who in one way or another here and now stand in need of liberation.

The scale and character of communal diakonia will be related to whether it is the parish community, the diocese, the national church or the universal church of which we are thinking. But each of these must be involved in one way or another if it is, at its proper level, to be the church. Again the choice of diakonia will relate to the size, the weight which a particular church has within its own secular society. A campaign for the abolition of slavery was not a viable form of diakonia for the first century church, but it was a long overdue form for the nineteenth century church. The spirit of Christ, the willingness to risk oneself for others, the determination to liberate are the same, but the contemporary opportunities and priorities, the structural patterns required, the scale of involvement in the political vary vastly. Because it was not feasible for St. Paul to enter the political arena does not mean that it may not be obligatory today to do so.

Diakonia must not be patronising or paternalistic or dominating, as so much ecclesiastical charitable and development work has been. It is not offered from a position of superiority, nor by those who do not need it themselves. Again, neither the kerygma nor the diakonia must be possessive. In the kerygma it is not our own truth we propose as against someone else's. The truth is above us, it judges us, and it sets us free while we proclaim it, just as it sets free those to whom we proclaim it. So too the diakonia, while it cannot help but somehow insinuate the kerygma and prepare men for a believing fellowship, must not be possessive and it must not be imperialist or domesticating. The service offered, the development work planned and executed by the church must not be aimed at enlisting people into our own society, at extending an ecclesial system, an offering of medicine in exchange for commitment. It is service to the human being and the human community offered in the spirit of service – without strings attached.

A diakonal kerygma, a kerygmatic diakonia; separate them and in christian terms they become invalid, inauthentic. But together they constitute mission – Christ's mission to the world which is the church's supreme responsibility, without which the church would simply not be. But each implies and further produces that third essential – communion, koinonia. Mission flows into fellowship, just as fellowship flows into mission. The church is essentially a kerygmatic communion, a diakonal communion; and the more kerygmatic and diakonal the communion is, the more will it be an unambiguous sign to the world and the more will it in fact draw men into the warmth and strength of its shared concern.

Koinonia, kerygma, diakonia, these three form the irreducible triangle of the church, like a hoe, a tool with three corners. Sometimes we will dig more with one angle, sometimes with another. At times it is the kerygma which must be brought strongly to the fore, at times the diakonia, at times the koinonia. But each in fact to be authentic must be supported by the other two corners.

The church is koinonia. She is communion, a fellowship, a society of friends. Here again the church as it exists at a particular time and place cannot wholly fail to be what it claims to be and should be. It can never not be communion. And yet it can greatly fail to be a communion. The existence and presence of the institutional church, the formal bond of hierarchical communion, even the regular celebration of the sacrament of communion, are all far from sufficient proof of the existence of a credible koinonia. The institutional church can indeed exist in a manner which only too clearly denies fellowship. The church has every day to become what it claims to be, both at the level of sacrament and at the level of spirit.

The fellowship is manifested above all in eating the common bread, sharing the common cup. The church's fellowship is a flowing out on all the sides of life from that central and focal point at which the supreme relevance of things happening two thousand years ago is most extraordinarily and most unequivocally reaffirmed. This koinonia is a human fellowship in which there is neither man nor woman, neither slave nor free, neither Jew nor Gentile, but all are one in Christ – not only one in the spirit but one in the flesh. The church is seen here at its central and starting point, at this moment when its very meaning is laid bare and affirmed, to be not primarily a spiritual and other-worldly reality, but a fleshly and earthly reality, an eating and drinking society, and so the body of the Lord. This, in the early days, was St. Peter's way of defining the group from which the church had grown: 'We who ate and drank with him after he rose from the dead'. That is what we have gone on doing and it is in a way the only thing we really need to do together. If we do this aright, all else would follow. We are then a physical society; as sacrament the church clearly must be so – a sign within the earthly, physical order of a fellowship in truth and love that goes far beyond all eating and drinking. To have a spiritual unity but a physical division would nullify the nature of the church because it would nullify the nature of a sacrament, destroy the sense of the eucharist and reject the lesson of the first great crisis in christian history. For this is the continuing message of that first great crisis culminating at Antioch: one cannot maintain a spiritual unity with physical apartness. In one of his short stories Rudyard Kipling put the point very well, describing the scene as follows: " 'But still', Petrus leaned forward like a deaf man, 'if we admitted Hebrew and Greek Christians to separate tables, we should escape' .... 'Nothing except salvation', said Paulus. 'We have broken with the whole law of Moses, you yourself have eaten with Gentiles, you yourself have said .... 'One says more than one means when one is carried away', Petrus answered, and his face worked again.

'This time you will say precisely what is meant', Paulus spoke between his teeth: 'We will keep the churches one. You dare not deny this ... Tomorrow you will speak to the one church of the one table the world over.' "

This was the most normative crisis for the church for all subsequent history: 'The one church of the one table the world over.' The 'one table' cannot be merely at the moment of the eucharist, but it has to be especially manifest at that moment, for the eucharist is the epitome of the church – of koinonia, of kerygma, of diakonia. Here is the fellowship, the common table, the shared cup; here is the proclamation: as often as you do this you proclaim the death of the Lord; here is service, the feeding of all who come. The eucharist expresses a fact, what the church is, but it also declares a programme, what the church should be. It says: Go out and be this, be a true fellowship of people of every sort, a serving fellowship, a proclaiming fellowship: a living memorial of the Lord.